Cambridge Elements ☰

Elements in Philosophy and Logic
edited by
Bradley Armour-Garb
SUNY Albany
Frederick Kroon
The University of Auckland

PROPOSITIONAL QUANTIFIERS

Peter Fritz
University of Oslo

CAMBRIDGE
UNIVERSITY PRESS

Shaftesbury Road, Cambridge CB2 8EA, United Kingdom

One Liberty Plaza, 20th Floor, New York, NY 10006, USA

477 Williamstown Road, Port Melbourne, VIC 3207, Australia

314–321, 3rd Floor, Plot 3, Splendor Forum, Jasola District Centre, New Delhi – 110025, India

103 Penang Road, #05–06/07, Visioncrest Commercial, Singapore 238467

Cambridge University Press is part of Cambridge University Press & Assessment, a department of the University of Cambridge.

We share the University's mission to contribute to society through the pursuit of education, learning and research at the highest international levels of excellence.

www.cambridge.org
Information on this title: www.cambridge.org/9781009532747

DOI: 10.1017/9781009177740

First published 2024

A catalogue record for this publication is available from the British Library.

ISBN 978-1-009-53274-7 Hardback
ISBN 978-1-009-17773-3 Paperback
ISSN 2516-418X (online)
ISSN 2516-4171 (print)

Propositional Quantifiers

Elements in Philosophy and Logic

DOI: 10.1017/9781009177740
First published online: May 2024

Peter Fritz
University of Oslo

Author for correspondence: Peter Fritz, peter.fritz@ifikk.uio.no

Abstract: Propositional quantifiers are quantifiers binding proposition letters, understood as variables. This Element introduces propositional quantifiers and explains why they are especially interesting in the context of propositional modal logics. It surveys the main results on propositionally quantified modal logics which have been obtained in the literature, presents a number of open questions, and provides examples of applications of such logics to philosophical problems.

Keywords: modal logic, propositional quantifier, propositionally quantified modal logic, second-order propositional modal logic, sentential quantifier

ISBNs: 9781009532747 (HB), 9781009177733 (PB), 9781009177740 (OC)
ISSNs: 2516-418X (online), 2516-4171 (print)

Contents

1 Propositional Quantifiers

1.1 Introduction

The simplest languages of formal logic are propositional. These languages provide sentential letters and connectives with which we can represent, for example, the conditional structure of a sentence like the following:

(1) If you invented the smiley, then I am the pope.

Letting s stand for you inventing the smiley, p for me being the pope, and using $\rightarrow$ to represent the conditional in (1), this can be formalized as follows:

(2) $s \rightarrow p$

Other familiar sentential connectives, such as negation, conjunction, disjunction, and the biconditional can be treated similarly, for which I will use the symbols $\neg$, $\wedge$, $\vee$, and $\leftrightarrow$ respectively.

It is often supposed that the connectives just mentioned are truth-functional. For example, the truth-value of $\neg p$ is plausibly determined by the truth-value of p: $\neg p$ is true just in case p is false, and $\neg p$ is false just in case p is true. But many applications of propositional logics across different disciplines require sentential connectives which are not truth-functional. Standard examples involve modal and epistemic notions, such as the following two:

(3) Necessarily, Jupiter is a planet.
(4) Kushim believes correctly that barley is a grain.

Necessity and belief are not truth-functional: some but not all truths are necessary, and some but not all truths (and falsehoods) may be believed by a given agent. Nevertheless, it is straightforward to extend the language of propositional logic to capture these statements as well. For the first, it suffices to introduce a sentential operator $\square$ for necessity, and for the second, a sentential operator B_k for being believed by Kushim:

(5) $\square r$
(6) $B_k g \wedge g$

In (5) and (6), r stands for Jupiter being a planet, and g for barley being a grain. The study of logical systems with sentential operators which are not truth-functional is known as *modal logic*; see, for example, Hughes and Cresswell (1996) and Blackburn et al. (2001).

All three of the examples just mentioned are particular, as opposed to general. For example, (4) attributes to Kushim a particular (correct) belief. But in many cases, it is important to be able to use quantifiers to express generality. For example, we might want to say not just that *this* belief of Kushim's is correct, but that *all* of Kushim's beliefs are correct. Or, to put the same point slightly differently, we might want to say:

(7) Everything Kushim believes is true.

Similarly, instead of attributing necessity specifically to Jupiter being a planet, we might want to say generally that necessity is not trivial, in the sense that there are examples of necessities. That is:

(8) Something is necessary.

As a final illustration, note that when I say in (1) ("If you invented the smiley, then I am the pope") that I am the pope, I am simply saying something which is patently false. I could equally have said that I am the king or queen of England, or made any other absurd claim. More generally, I might say that any absurdity is the case, or simply – and absurdly – that everything is the case:

(9) If you invented the smiley, then everything is the case.

Standard propositional languages do not provide any quantifiers, so there is no useful way of regimenting these three quantified claims in these languages. But it would take little to allow for such quantification: We would only have to allow ourselves to use sentential letters like p, q, and r as variables, and to bind them by a universal quantifier $\forall$ and an existential quantifier $\exists$, analogous to the familiar case of the quantifiers of first-order logic which bind individual variables. With such quantifiers, (7), (8), and (9) are straightforwardly formalized as follows:

(10) $\forall p(B_k p \rightarrow p)$
(11) $\exists p \Box p$
(12) $s \rightarrow \forall q\, q$

Logic is not just about formalizing statements, but also about capturing logical properties of, and relationships among, such statements. For example, (3) ("Necessarily, Jupiter is a planet") is an instance of the existential claim (8) ("Something is necessary"), and so the latter follows intuitively from the former. Thus, we would expect $\exists p \Box p$ to be counted as a logical consequence of $\Box r$. Using instances of classical propositional reasoning, this follows straightforwardly by a schematic principle of existential introduction, in particular the following instance:

(13) $\Box r \to \exists p \Box p$

Analogously, $s \to p$ can be obtained from $s \to \forall q\, q$ using the following instance of universal instantiation:

(14) $\forall q\, q \to p$

By classical propositional reasoning, $s \to \forall q\, q$ and $\forall q\, q \to p$ give us $s \to p$, as required.

Such quantifiers, binding variables which occupy the position of formulas, are often called *propositional quantifiers*, for example by Kripke (1959) and Fine (1970). This Element is about these quantifiers in the context of propositional languages, their logic, and their applications in philosophy. This introductory Section 1 explains first, in Section 1.2, why the job of propositional quantifiers cannot obviously be done by the more familiar quantifiers of first-order logic. Section 1.3 gives a partial explanation of why propositional quantifiers are rarely encountered: in the context of many logical systems, they are redundant in at least one of two different senses of redundancy. Section 1.4 explains why there is nevertheless a range of interesting settings in which propositional quantifiers are not redundant, and in which they are usefully studied. The main examples for this are propositional modal languages along the lines mentioned earlier. Consequently, the following Sections 2 and 3 of this Element are concerned with the resulting propositionally quantified modal logics. Section 1.5 provides an outlook on these sections and explains why they are structured according to different styles of set-theoretic model theories for such logics. A final Section 1.6 of the present section gives a brief overview of the historical development of propositional quantifiers in formal logic.

This Element presents a continuous narrative, but it is also possible to read the various sections selectively and out of order. Figure 1 presents a dependency diagram indicating which sections depend on which other sections. The label "PML" indicates that starting with Section 2, familiarity with the basics of propositional modal logic will be assumed. The central logical theory of propositionally quantified modal logics is developed in the section numbers highlighted in bold.

1.2 Why Propositional Quantifiers?

Before we get any further into the theory of propositional quantifiers, it is worth considering why one might want to use these quantifiers in the first place. In many contexts, quantificational claims can be captured straightforwardly using first-order logic, which is an extremely well-understood and very well-behaved

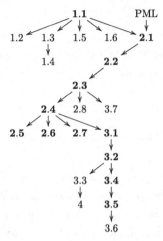

Figure 1 Dependency among sections

formal system. Can't we just use first-order logic to formalize the preceding examples?

In first-order logic, an atomic formula consists of an application of a predicate F to a finite number of arguments $t_1, \ldots, t_n$, forming the statement $Ft_1 \ldots t_n$. In the simplest case, the arguments are individual variables $x_1, \ldots, x_n$, which can be bound by first-order quantifiers $\forall$ and $\exists$. Thus, the claim that every echidna is happy can be formalized as follows, with the obvious interpretations of the predicate letters:

(15) $\forall x(Ex \rightarrow Hx)$

How might we use such first-order quantifiers to formalize, for example, (8) ("Something is necessary")? We cannot just replace a propositional variable by a first-order variable: $\square$ is a sentential operator, and so $\square$ can only be applied to formulas, and not to individual variables; thus the string $\exists x \square x$ is ill-formed. There are two natural options to overcome this difficulty. First, we might use a necessity *predicate* N instead of a necessity *operator* $\square$. With N, we might use the following formula of first-order logic:

(16) $\exists xNx$

Second, we might introduce a truth predicate T. We can then attribute necessity to x by stating that x is necessarily true. With T, we might then use the following formula of first-order modal logic:

(17) $\exists x \square Tx$

Consider first the option of using modal predicates. Using a predicate N instead of a sentential operator $\square$ has a knock-on effect for the formalization of particular necessity claims. As noted, we want our formalization to capture that (8) ("Something is necessary") follows from (3) ("Necessarily, Jupiter is a planet"). But it is not clear how $\exists x N x$ could be seen to be a logical consequence of $\square r$. The obvious response to this difficulty is to reconsider the formalization of (3), and use N instead of $\square$. However, we can again not simply exchange N and $\square$, since they take different types of expressions as arguments. In order to be able to apply N, Jupiter being a planet must be expressed by an individual term instead of a formula.

The problem would be solved if we could turn any formula, such as Fj, into a corresponding individual term. A natural idea is therefore to introduce a device which effects this transformation. So, let us consider an extension of the language of first-order logic in which for every formula φ, there is an individual term $[\varphi]$. For example, (3) ("Necessarily, Jupiter is a planet") can then be formalized in more detail as follows:

(18) $N[Fj]$

Now, $\exists x N x$ follows straightforwardly from $N[Fj]$ using existential introduction in first-order logic.

On the modal predicate approach, there are also cases which call out for a truth predicate. Consider (7) ("Everything Kushim believes is true"). As in the previous case, we might use a first-order quantifier instead of a propositional quantifier, and a predicate K instead of the sentential operator B_k to capture the notion of being believed by Kushim. With this, we can state that Kushim believes something using the formula $\exists x K x$. But it is not possible to formalize (7) along the lines of $\forall p(B_k p \rightarrow p)$; in particular, the string $\forall x(Kx \rightarrow x)$ is ill-formed, since x cannot take the position of a formula. The simplest way to address this deficiency is to introduce a truth predicate T. We can then propose to use the following formula:

(19) $\forall x(Kx \rightarrow Tx)$

The truth predicate T serves as something of an inverse of the propositional abstraction device $[\ldots]$ with which we obtain an individual term $[\varphi]$ from a formula φ: The first turns an individual term into a corresponding formula, and the second turns a formula into a corresponding individual term.

Thus, the modal predicate approach leads us to introducing a truth predicate. But, as we have seen, with a truth predicate we could also avoid introducing modal predicates and write, for example, $\square Tx$ instead of Nx. It is also instructive to consider the inferential relationships between the various claims on this second approach. To capture that (8) ("Something is necessary") follows from (3) ("Necessarily, Jupiter is a planet"), we now would want $\exists x \Box Tx$ to follow from $\Box r$. Again, this means going from a sentential expression r to an individual variable x, which is naturally effected using the propositional abstraction device [. . .]. For example, one might appeal to the following schematic principle governing truth, where φ may be any formula:

(20) $\varphi \leftrightarrow T[\varphi]$

(This principle is closely related to the schematic biconditionals discussed by Tarski [1983 [1933]], but note that the latter deal with sentences rather than propositions.) Let φ be r, and consider the left-to-right direction: $r \to T[r]$. By standard axiomatic modal reasoning, using the rule of necessitation and the distributivity axiom for $\Box$, if $r \to T[r]$ is derivable, then so is $\Box r \to \Box T[r]$. From $\Box r$, we therefore obtain $\Box T[r]$, and so $\exists x \Box Tx$ by existential introduction.

Thus, although we can use first-order quantifiers instead of propositional quantifiers, both of the ways of doing so sketched here require further logical resources, in particular a truth predicate T and the propositional abstraction device [. . .]. One of them allows us to continue to use modal operators, as standard in modal logic; the other replaces them with modal predicates. It is worth noting that one might also endorse a hybrid approach which provides both modal operators and modal predicates; this could be justified by arguing that there is a philosophically important distinction between "necessarily" and "necessary" which gets conflated in standard uses of modal logic.

We have seen that there are ways of formalizing the quantificational examples of Section 1.1 in first-order logic. However, I hope to have illustrated that they come with certain complexities. In contrast, formalizations using propositional quantifiers are extremely simple. The complexities of first-order approaches may earn their keep by allowing for the formulation of theories which do better on other dimensions of theoretical virtue. This is not the place to try to settle these issues. For defenses of different versions of the first-order approach, see Halbach and Welch (2009) and Bealer (1998); for exchanges on the relative merits of the first-order and propositional approaches, see Anderson (1987) and Bealer (1994), as well as Menzel (2024) and Williamson (2024).

One straightforward reason for investigating propositional quantifiers is therefore their simplicity. Another has to do with the ontological commitments of different forms of quantification. When we regiment claims like (8) ("Something is necessary") using first-order quantifiers, it is natural to take these quantifiers to range over propositions. Existential claims like $\exists x Nx$ and $\exists x \Box Tx$ therefore commit us to an ontology of propositions, namely to the existence of certain things – propositions – which are necessary. Nominalists, according to whom there are no propositions, will disagree with this claim. They might instead appeal to propositional quantifiers and argue that there is a way of interpreting the existential propositional quantification $\exists p\Box p$ which makes it an existential generalization of $\Box r$, without entailing the existence of propositions. On this view, propositional quantifiers should *not* be understood as ranging over propositions. How, then, should they be understood? According to one version of this view, propositional quantifiers should be thought of as a new, sui generis, form of quantification. In informal discussion, we might still paraphrase them using the available English constructions, but these paraphrases should – in the words of Frege (1892) – be taken with a grain of salt. Alternatively, we could introduce into English new constructions which better correspond to propositional quantifiers, as suggested by Prior (1971, section 3.4) and Grover (1972). In any case, on this use of logics with propositional quantifiers, there is a sense in which propositional quantifiers do not quantify over propositions. For more on these kinds of views, see Fritz and Jones (2024).

In order to avoid suggesting that propositional quantifiers quantify over propositions, such quantifiers are sometimes also called "sentential quantifiers"; see, for example, Künne (2003). Although this label brings out clearly that the relevant quantifiers bind variables which take *sentential* position, it also invites the suggestion that they are quantifiers ranging over sentences. In many cases, this would be a misunderstanding. There are *substitutional* readings of propositional quantifiers, and model-theoretic constructions in which the truth-conditions of propositional quantifiers are specified in terms of metatheoretic quantification over sentences; such approaches will be discussed in Section 3.7. But unless it is explicitly indicated that such a reading is intended, propositional (sentential) quantifiers should also not be taken as ranging over sentences.

1.3 Redundancy

I have argued that propositional quantifiers are natural and useful logical concepts, which cannot straightforwardly be replaced by more familiar forms of quantification in formal logic. Yet, propositional quantifiers are relatively underexplored. In this section, we observe one important reason for this: in many contexts, propositional quantifiers are redundant in at least one of two senses of redundancy.

To illustrate the first sense of redundancy, consider classical propositional logic. Assume that the formulation of this logic under consideration includes two logical sentential constants, $\top$ and $\bot$, with $\top$ and $\neg\bot$ being provable.

Since all sentential operators of classical propositional logic are truth-functional, any two materially equivalent formulas can be replaced, salva veritate, in any context. In this sense, classical propositional logic is *extensional*. Because of this, we can simulate propositional quantification straightforwardly: A universal quantification $\forall p \varphi$ is true just in case φ is true under any interpretation of p. By extensionality, since only the truth-value of φ matters, this is the case if and only if φ is true when p is replaced by $\top$ or $\bot$, for which we will write $\varphi[\top/p]$ and $\varphi[\bot/p]$, respectively. Instead of $\forall p \varphi$, we can therefore simply write $\varphi[\top/p] \wedge \varphi[\bot/p]$. Similarly, instead of $\exists p \varphi$, we can write $\varphi[\top/p] \vee \varphi[\bot/p]$.

The argument just sketched is essentially semantic, as it appeals to interpretations of the proposition letters. It is worth noting that a more careful version of the argument can be carried out deductively, using the principles of classical propositional logic and standard principles of elementary quantification for propositional quantifiers. The argument also extends to many other extensional logics, including classical first-order logic, second-order logic, and any extensions of these systems by generalized quantifiers: in all of them, adding propositional quantifiers is redundant along the lines sketched earlier. It will therefore be worth developing this argument a little more carefully and generally. We focus only on the universal propositional quantifier; the argument for the existential propositional quantifier is analogous and can also be derived from the universal case on the assumption that one quantifier is the dual of the other.

Let $\mathcal{L}^*$ be a logical language, the formulas of which are defined by a standard recursion, and let $\vdash^*$ be a proof system for $\mathcal{L}^*$. We write $\vdash^* \varphi$ for a formula φ of $\mathcal{L}^*$ being provable in $\vdash^*$. We assume the following:

- We have defined the notion of an occurrence of a propositional variable p being *free* in a formula φ, and the notion of a formula ψ being *free for* a propositional variable p in a formula φ. (These are standard notions of logical systems; see Section 2.1 for definitions in the case of propositionally quantified modal logic.) If the latter condition is satisfied, we write $\varphi[\psi/p]$ for the result of replacing every free occurrence of p in φ by ψ.
- $\mathcal{L}^*$ is closed under the Boolean connectives, including $\top$ and $\bot$, as well as the universal propositional quantifier $\forall p$, so that $\forall p \varphi$ is a formula whenever φ is a formula.
- The formulas provable in $\vdash^*$ include all classical tautologies and are closed under modus ponens (MP), the rule that if $\vdash^* \varphi$ and $\vdash^* \varphi \rightarrow \psi$, then $\vdash^* \psi$.
- $\vdash^*$ includes the principles of *universal instantiation* (UI) and *universal generalization* (UG) for propositional quantifiers. So, if ψ is free for p in φ, then

$\vdash^* \forall p\varphi \rightarrow \varphi[\psi/p],$

and if p is not free in φ, then

$\vdash^* \varphi \rightarrow \psi$ only if $\vdash^* \varphi \rightarrow \forall p\psi$.

- $\mathcal{L}^*$ is *extensional* according to $\vdash^*$, in the sense that whenever ψ and χ are free for p in φ, then:

  $\vdash^* (\psi \leftrightarrow \chi) \rightarrow (\varphi[\psi/p] \leftrightarrow \varphi[\chi/p])$

It follows from these assumptions that the formulas provable in $\vdash^*$ are closed under uniform substitution, in the sense that $\varphi[\psi/p]$ is provable whenever φ is provable and ψ is free for p in φ; the argument is analogous to the proof of Proposition 2.2.2.

The elimination of propositional quantifiers can be stated more rigorously by defining a mapping $\cdot^*$ from $\mathcal{L}^*$ to the sublanguage of $\mathcal{L}^*$ in which no universal propositional quantifiers occur. This mapping is defined recursively, with only one nontrivial clause:

$$(\forall p\varphi)^* := \varphi^*[\top/p] \wedge \varphi^*[\bot/p]$$

To say that the mapping is recursive and all other cases are trivial is just to say that $\top^* := \top$, $(\neg\varphi)^* := \neg(\varphi^*)$, and so on.

We can now prove that this elimination succeeds by showing that it maps any formula to a provably equivalent formula which does not contain any universal propositional quantifiers:

Claim For every formula $\varphi \in \mathcal{L}^*$, $\vdash^* \varphi \leftrightarrow \varphi^*$.

Argument The argument is by induction on the complexity of φ. By the construction of the mapping $\cdot^*$, it suffices to consider just the case of universal propositional quantifiers, and show that $\vdash^* \forall p\varphi \leftrightarrow (\forall p\varphi)^*$ on the assumption that $\vdash^* \varphi \leftrightarrow \varphi^*$. We consider the two directions of the biconditional separately.

For the left-to-right direction, note first that by UI, tautologies, and MP,

$\vdash^* \forall p\varphi \rightarrow \varphi[\top/p] \wedge \varphi[\bot/p].$

Second, by induction hypothesis (IH), $\vdash^* \varphi \rightarrow \varphi^*$. So, for $+$ being $\top$ or $\bot$, it follows by uniform substitution that

$\vdash^* \varphi[+/p] \rightarrow \varphi^*[+/p].$

Using tautologies and MP, we obtain, from these two observations,

$\vdash^* \forall p\varphi \rightarrow \varphi^*[\top/p] \wedge \varphi^*[\bot/p].$

This is $\vdash^* \forall p\varphi \rightarrow (\forall p\varphi)^*$, as required.

For the right-to-left direction, note first the following two instances of extensionality:

$$\vdash^* (p \leftrightarrow \top) \rightarrow (\varphi^* \leftrightarrow \varphi^*[\top/p])$$
$$\vdash^* (p \leftrightarrow \bot) \rightarrow (\varphi^* \leftrightarrow \varphi^*[\bot/p])$$

By tautologies and MP, we conclude:

$$\vdash^* \varphi^*[\top/p] \wedge \varphi^*[\bot/p] \rightarrow \varphi^*$$

By IH, $\vdash^* \varphi^* \rightarrow \varphi$, and so:

$$\vdash^* \varphi^*[\top/p] \wedge \varphi^*[\bot/p] \rightarrow \varphi$$

Since p is not free in the antecedent of this conditional, we can apply UG:

$$\vdash^* \varphi^*[\top/p] \wedge \varphi^*[\bot/p] \rightarrow \forall p\varphi,$$

which is $\vdash^* (\forall p\varphi)^* \rightarrow \forall p\varphi$, as required. This concludes the argument.

It is routine to show that many standard logical systems, including classical propositional logic, first-order logic, and second-order logic, all satisfy the assumptions of this result when propositional quantifiers are added to the syntax and the deductive principles UI and UG are added to a standard axiomatic proof system. The crucial condition of extensionality can be shown by induction on the complexity of formulas. In all these logics, propositional quantifiers are therefore redundant in the sense that they can be eliminated along the lines developed here.

The eliminability of propositional quantifiers shows that for many purposes, it is pointless to add propositional quantifiers. However, not every property one may be interested in is preserved under the elimination. Most importantly, the elimination of propositional quantifiers leads to an exponential increase in the size of formulas. Consequently, the elimination of propositional quantifiers may not preserve matters of computational complexity of the logic in question. This can be illustrated by the basic case of classical propositional logic. The problem of determining whether a formula of classical propositional logic is satisfiable (i.e., is true under some assignment of truth values to the proposition letters) is NP-complete, whereas the corresponding satisfiability problem for classical propositional logic with propositional quantifiers is PSPACE-complete. (For further details, including definitions of these complexity classes, see Blackburn et al. [2001, pp. 514–516]. That PSPACE-completeness comes apart from NP-completeness is conjectured, but has not been proven.) Classical propositional logic with propositional quantifiers is also known as QBF ("quantified Boolean formulas"); for applications in artificial intelligence and related fields, see Shukla et al. (2019). There are also applications of propositional quantifiers to the axiomatics of classical propositional logic; we discuss them in Section 1.6.

In second-order logic, propositional quantifiers can also be seen to be redundant in a second sense: Second-order logic adds to first-order logic variables taking the position of predicates, and quantifiers binding these variables. For example, in second-order logic, we can state $\forall X(Xc)$. For a detailed introduction to second-order logic, see Shapiro (1991). Just as predicate constants can have any arity, so can second-order variables. Depending on the formulation of second-order logic, this may not just include the cases of polyadic and monadic variables, but also the limiting case of zero-adic, or *nullary*, variables. A nullary predicate takes no arguments to form an atomic predication, so we can understand it as a propositional constant. Analogously, a nullary second-order variable can be understood as a propositional variable. Propositional quantifiers can therefore be understood as nullary second-order quantifiers. In the context of a suitable formulation of second-order logic, propositional quantifiers are therefore also redundant in a second sense: they are already included.

The second sense of redundancy extends to higher-order extensions of second-order logic. This is important since third- and higher-order logics do not (without further assumptions) satisfy the extensionality requirement of the first redundancy argument. This is easy to see: In third-order logic, a standard predicate F can not only be applied to individual terms to form an atomic formula, but also serve itself as the argument of a (higher-order) predicate Y. Here, Y may be a constant or a variable; if it is a variable, it may also be bound by a quantifier. To illustrate, in this case we may construct a formula $\forall Y(YF \rightarrow \forall xFx)$. Since propositional variables p and q can be understood as nullary second-order variables, there is a third-order variable X which takes p or q as an argument. Consider now the following claim:

$$(p \leftrightarrow q) \rightarrow (Xp \leftrightarrow Xq)$$

Although p and q might have the same truth-value, the two variables need not stand for the same proposition. Thus one of them might have a property X which the other lacks. This is an informal semantic argument, but it can easily be turned into a rigorous model-theoretic proof to show that in third- and higher-order logic (without any extensionality assumptions), this instance of the extensionality schema cannot be derived. In this sense, the step from second- to third- and higher-order logic takes us outside the realm of extensionality. In third- and higher-order logic, propositional quantifiers are therefore not redundant in the first sense, but they are redundant in the second sense:

while they are not eliminable, they are already included as nullary second-order quantifiers.

1.4 Fragments of Higher-Order Logic

The two arguments for redundancy discussed in the last section explain why it is often uninteresting to add propositional quantifiers to a given logical language: If the language is sufficiently restrictive to be extensional, like propositional, first-order, and second-order logic, propositional quantifiers are eliminable. If the language is sufficiently inclusive, like second-, third-, and higher-order logic, then propositional quantifiers are already included as nullary second-order quantifiers. In fact, it may seem that these two arguments cover all interesting logical systems. But this is not so.

There are logics which are non-extensional without incorporating full third- or higher-order logic. The most well-known cases are propositional modal logics, which add to the language of classical propositional logic one or more (non-truth-functional) sentential operators. Such operators can be understood as third-order constants, taking nullary second-order variables (i.e., propositional variables) and complex terms of the same syntactic type (i.e., formulas) as arguments. If we ignore the difference between variables and constants – which is immaterial in the absence of quantifiers – the languages of propositional modal logics can therefore be seen as certain quantifier-free fragments of the languages of third-order logic. (One might object that third-order constants are non-logical, whereas modal operators are logical. But in practice, it is not easy to see what this difference should amount to, especially as modal logics are used in a variety of different applications, on different interpretations of the modal operators.)

If the languages of propositional modal logic are fragments of the language of third-order logic, then so are their extensions by propositional quantifiers: they can be understood as obtained by adding to the relevant quantifier-free fragment the special case of nullary second-order quantifiers. In such a context, propositional quantifiers need not be redundant in either of the two senses discussed earlier: the first redundancy argument does not apply, since propositional modal logics are typically not extensional, and the second redundancy argument does not apply since they do not already include propositional quantifiers (or any other form of quantification).

One might wonder: Why bother with all these fragments? Why not just work in third-, or better, higher-order logic? In some cases, this may well be the best option, but it will not be the best option in all cases. Third- and higher-order logics are complex systems, which may well introduce significant complications.

If the full flexibility of these systems is not required, it may well be a significant advantage to make do with a more restrictive fragment. For example, many second- and higher-order logics are essentially incomplete: the valid formulas, on a suitable notion of validity, cannot be exactly captured by any proof system. In technical terms, the validities are not recursively enumerable, essentially due to the incompleteness results of Gödel (1931). By restricting the language to the formulas of a propositional modal logic, this issue is very often avoided, as very many propositional modal logics are computationally much more tractable.

In systematically investigating the principles of a logic of, for example, belief, there are therefore good reasons not to always work in full higher-order logic, but sometimes also in more restrictive fragments, like propositional logic with an extra unary sentential operator. In some cases, however, the restrictions of this particular fragment may prove to be too limiting. Our initial examples, such as (7) ("Everything Kushim believes is true"), illustrate this, showing that in many applications, it is natural to quantify over the arguments of modalities. Such quantification does not require the full power of third-order logic: we can expand propositional modal logic more carefully using just the required propositional (i.e., nullary second-order) quantifiers. As we will see later in this Element, in some but not all cases, such quantifiers preserve the tractability of propositional modal logics. Just like propositional modal logics, their extensions by propositional quantifiers provide a trade-off between strength and tractability. Which systems are most suitable will depend on the particular application.

Propositional modal logics are the main setting in which propositional quantifiers have been studied, and they will also be the focus of this Element. But there are other settings in which they play an important role. In particular, there are other proper fragments of third- and higher-order logics which include propositional quantifiers, and in which they are not eliminable. For example, propositional quantifiers can be added to first-order modal logic. Such a language has proven useful in investigating the interpolation property in first-order modal logics; see the discussion of Fine (1979) by Kripke (1983), as well as Fitting (2002). Another example is the extension of modal logics by propositional quantifiers and third-order quantifiers binding variables in the position of sentential operators. A philosophical application of such a system can be found in Fritz (2023c).

In the following, I will call a propositional modal logic with propositional quantifiers a "propositionally quantified modal logic". In the literature, this label is used interchangeably with "quantified propositional modal logic". The reason for adopting the former rather than the latter is that the former makes clear that only propositional quantifiers added. Logics with further quantifiers are therefore explicitly excluded, such as the one just mentioned which incorporates certain third-order quantifiers.

1.5 Outlook

For the reasons discussed in the previous subsection, the two subsequent sections of this Element will focus on propositional quantifiers in the context of propositional modal logic. It makes little sense to consider such extensions without having already studied propositional modal logics on their own. Consequently, from Section 2 on, I will assume familiarity with basic definitions and results in propositional modal logic.

The material to be discussed in the remaining two sections is organized according to different model-theoretic approaches. The main reason for this is a matter of expository convenience: different model-theoretic approaches require rather different mathematical tools. The sections aim to introduce the relevant model-theoretic concepts, to consider the logics to which the relevant models give rise from a deductive perspective, and to illustrate the usefulness of these ideas in applications. For reasons of space, it will only be possible to *state* many of the most important results; in these cases, proofs can be found in the references provided. This Element therefore aims to be an introduction and a survey rather than a comprehensive textbook on propositional quantifiers. Although many interesting results have been obtained on propositionally quantified modal logics, many natural questions have not been considered. A number of basic results on such questions will be established here; in these cases, proofs are either routine or are provided in detail. Many further questions remain open, and many specific results await a more systematic treatment. Each section therefore also states some important open questions concerning the relevant model-theoretic approach.

Section 2 discusses the most well-known models for propositional modal logic, based on sets of possible worlds and relations of accessibility between them; such structures are known as *relational frames* or *Kripke frames*. On such frames, propositional quantifiers can be interpreted straightforwardly as ranging over sets of worlds. Section 2.1 begins by laying out the syntax of propositionally quantified modal logics. Section 2.2 sets up proof systems in a general manner, and formulates the axioms and rules of classical logic for propositional quantifiers. Section 2.3 introduces relational frames and the resulting notion of normality for modal logics. To illustrate the usefulness of propositional quantifiers in applications, this section also briefly discusses the knowability paradox, and shows how its conclusion can be derived formally using the proof systems defined here. Section 2.4 considers two further principles which are valid on relational frames, namely a version of the Barcan formula and a principle of *atomicity* which is unique to the case of propositional quantifiers. Section 2.5 discusses the well-known modal logic S5, in which propositional quantifiers behave especially well, and lead to an axiomatizable logic. As a second illustration of an application of propositional quantifiers, this section also discusses arguments to the effect that possible worlds can be understood as special propositions, and shows how these arguments might be formalized using propositional quantifiers. Section 2.6 turns to the more technical question of (recursive) axiomatizability of propositionally quantified modal logics on classes of relational frames, and notes that propositional quantifiers often lead to unaxiomatizability. Only in relatively few cases is it possible to give complete axiomatizations; these cases and the corresponding completeness questions are discussed in Section 2.7. The final Section 2.8 discusses some model-theoretic beginnings, focusing in particular on transformations of relational frames and their interactions with propositional quantifiers.

Section 3 turns to interpretations of propositionally quantified modal languages beyond relational frames. Section 3.1 begins by generalizing relational frames to neighborhood frames, which are still based on possible worlds. Section 3.2 goes further and generalizes neighborhood frames to models based on complete Boolean algebras. Section 3.3 discusses a generalization which can be applied to any frames based on possible worlds or models based on complete Boolean algebras, which is to distinguish either one of the worlds, or a filter of the algebra. Section 3.4 discusses a second way of generalizing models based on complete Boolean algebras, namely by weakening the requirement for the algebra to be complete. Section 3.5 considers the corresponding generalization of relational and neighborhood frames, which involves limiting which sets of possible worlds are counted as propositions. All of the generalizations of these five sections are well-known in the case of propositional modal logics, but many of them have been little explored in the presence of propositional quantifiers. Section 3.6 considers possible worlds models in which the domain of propositional quantification varies from world to world, adapting well-known model-theoretic ideas for modal predicate logic. Section 3.7 notes that propositional quantifiers need not be interpreted as ranging over any domain of propositions at all, as there are formally coherent ways of interpreting propositional quantifiers as substitutional, and so as ranging – in some sense – over sentences. The final Section 4 notes that even if propositional quantifiers are interpreted as ranging over a domain of propositions supplied by a model, and the model is to validate the principles of classical logic, the domain of quantification does not have to constitute a Boolean algebra. It concludes by using propositional quantifiers to discuss certain paradoxes of propositional attitudes and propositional individuation. A list of abbreviations is included at the end.

The brief discussion of non-Boolean models in Section 4 also points to the biggest omission of this Element: we will not consider propositional quantifiers in the context of nonclassical propositional logics. The argument for the eliminability of propositional quantifiers in Section 1.3 depends on the principles of classical logic. In certain nonclassical systems, including intuitionistic and relevant logics, propositional quantifiers cannot be eliminated from propositional logic even without any additional modal operators. Apart from the study of propositional quantifiers in the context of propositional modal logics, their most detailed investigations in the literature can be found in the context of such nonclassical logics. Although for reasons of space, these nonclassical investigations will not be discussed in this Element, references to the relevant literature can be found at the end of the next section.

1.6 Historical Overview

While later sections will make references to the relevant literature, the aim there will be to present the state of the art, rather than to proceed historically. It will therefore be useful to provide some historical context, both on earlier developments and on important motivating applications.

Early Work (1879–1955) The theory of quantification in modern symbolic logic goes back to the *Begriffsschrift* of Frege (1879). The syntax of Frege's system is not defined rigorously, but the introduction of quantifiers by Frege (1879, p. 19) is plausibly general enough to encompass propositional quantification. Indeed, Frege employs propositional quantifiers himself in correspondence with Russell from 1904; see Frege (1980, pp. 158–166). The use Russell and Frege make of propositional quantifiers is interesting: They discuss a proposal by Russell to define negation by letting $\neg\varphi$ stand for $\varphi \rightarrow \forall pp$. It is now not uncommon to define $\neg\varphi$ as standing for $\varphi \rightarrow \bot$, and we can think of Russell's proposal as combining this with a definition of $\bot$ as $\forall pp$. Effectively, this defines the contradictory $\bot$ as standing for the claim that everything is the case. Although it may initially seem odd to define the negation of a statement φ as the claim that φ materially implies a contradiction, we have already seen in the first example (1) ("If you invented the smiley, then I am the pope") that something very similar is felicitous in English. In his letter, Frege hesitates to endorse Russell's definition of negation, but his reservations concern only the relative priority of the relevant connectives, and not the intelligibility of propositional quantification, which Frege notes is easily expressed in the notation of his *Begriffsschrift*.

Shortly after this correspondence, propositional quantifiers occur in published work by Russell (1906, p. 192). However, Russell quickly moves from a higher-order logic along the lines sketched in Section 1.4 to a much more complicated system, the *ramified type theory* of Russell (1908) and Whitehead and Russell (1910–13). Although ramified systems still contain quantifiers which can be understood as propositional quantifiers, they are all in a certain sense restricted; in this sense, these systems do not offer any unrestricted propositional quantifiers. Russell's evolving views on logic – including propositional quantification – can be traced through his published and unpublished writings in this period, which are now available as Russell (2014).

An early philosophical application of propositional quantifiers occurs in the work of Frank Ramsey. Ramsey (1923, 1927) proposes a version of the deflationary theory of truth, according to which asserting that it is true that Caesar was murdered amounts to asserting that Caesar was murdered. Ramsey notes that such an elimination of the truth predicate is harder to effect in quantified contexts, such as the earlier example of (7) ("Everything Kushim believes is true"). However, Ramsey argues that this need for a truth predicate seems to be a peculiarity of English, and not an essential matter concerning truth: using a propositional *variable p*, we can state that that for every p, if Kushim believes p, then p. In unpublished work, Ramsey (1991, p. 9, note 7) makes a similar point explicitly using a propositional *quantifier*. Formalizing (7) using propositional quantifiers as (10), as proposed here, is therefore clearly in the spirit of Ramsey's proposal. Ramsey's deflationism is anticipated in posthumously published work, of 1904 by Brentano (1966, pp. 45–48) and of 1915 by Frege (1979, pp. 251–252), but neither of them uses any symbolism in these notes, and therefore also no propositional quantifiers.

A few years after Ramsey's discussion, propositional quantifiers play a significant role in the first edition of Lewis and Langford (1959 [1932], see ch. VI, sect. 6). Lewis and Langford develop proof systems for propositional modal logic, and note that they intend not to include the principle which may be rendered in modern notation as follows:

(21) $\Box(p \rightarrow q) \lor \Box(p \rightarrow \neg q)$

This is a version of the well-known principle of conditional excluded middle – see, for example, Lewis (1973, pp. 79–83) – for strict implication. Lewis and Langford note that they not only intend this principle not to be derivable, but in fact to assert that it has false instances. This motivates them to introduce propositional quantifiers, with which the relevant claim is straightforwardly made using a prefix of existential quantifiers binding p and q. Introducing standard principles of quantification for propositional quantifiers, they go on to derive various formulas of propositionally quantified modal logic. Among the derivable formulas is a version of our earlier example (11) in which □ is formulated as the dual of ◇, namely $\exists p\neg\Diamond\neg p$; see Lewis and Langford (1959 [1932], p. 185, 20.21). In other discussions of modal logic until the late 1950s, propositional quantifiers are rarely isolated. But in this period, modal logic is often developed in what would strike us today as very ambitious logical settings, in some cases including first- and second-order quantifiers, which, as noted in Section 1.3, subsume propositional quantifiers; for examples, see Barcan (1947), Carnap (1947, esp. pp. 45, 179, & 191–193), and Bayart (1958, 1959), the last of which are now available in translation and with commentary by Cresswell (2015).

The definability of ⊥ in terms of propositional quantifiers suggested by Russell's definition of negation may seem to be nothing more than a neat trick. But such definitions play an important role in the formulation of *protothetic*, a version of higher-order logic developed by Lesniewski (1929). Using also quantifiers binding variables in the position of unary sentential operators, Tajtelbaum-Tarski (1923) shows that conjunction, and so all other truth-functional connectives, are definable using just the biconditional connective and universal quantifiers. In general, propositional quantifiers are found in a number of early formulations of propositional logic, including one by Łukasiewicz and Tarski (1930). In subsequent years, considerable ingenuity is expended on finding the shortest axiomatization of classical propositional logic in the presence of suitable quantifiers, culminating in the discovery by Meredith (1951) of the sufficiency of the single axiom $oo\bot \rightarrow op$, with o an operator variable and ⊥ defined as $\forall pp$, building on work by Łukasiewicz (1951).

Systems of protothetic which include a suitable axiom, such as the *law of substitution* discussed by Tajtelbaum-Tarski (1923), are extensional in the sense of Section 1.3. This means that as long as a sufficient basis of truth-functional connectives is included, propositional quantifiers can be eliminated, as discussed by Church (1956, pp. 151–154) along the lines presented in Section 1.3. By the 1950s, protothetic and investigations of axiomatizations of classical propositional logic using propositional quantifiers are already out of step with the trajectory of symbolic logic. This sentiment is expressed clearly by Myhill (1957, p. 118), who, in a review of a textbook on logic by Prior (1955), criticizes Prior for devoting attention to such "bizarreries" as protothetic. Nevertheless, propositional quantifiers receive an explicit defense by Church (1962), and an extension of protothetic to a fuller propositional type hierarchy is discussed by Henkin (1963) and Andrews (1963), albeit only as a stepping stone toward developing new methods for a more standard higher-order logic.

Active Years (1955–1975) Starting in the late 1950s and continuing through the 1960s, great advances are made in the study of modal logic. As we have seen earlier, in such modal contexts, propositional quantifiers play a more substantial role, and it is therefore not surprising to see a renewed interest in propositional quantifiers in this period. Essentially, these investigations return to the applications of propositional quantifiers pioneered by Ramsey, and Lewis and Langford, some three decades earlier. This is not to say that no studies of propositional quantifiers in intensional systems are considered in this intervening period – see, for example, Łoś (1948), an English review of which was published by Suszko (1949) – but only that they did not seem to have elicited much excitement.

Arguably the most influential advocate of propositional quantifiers in the period of their resurgence is Arthur Prior. Prior (1955, pp. 190–192) already briefly discusses questions arising from the combination of propositional quantifiers and modal operators, addressing an argument of Łukasiewicz (1951). Two years later, Prior (1957) considers a range of interpretations of modal operators, including temporal, alethic, epistemic, and deontic ones. Prior (1957, pp. 130–131) briefly mentions an example involving propositional quantification into an epistemic context, which prompts Cohen (1957, p. 231, fn. 6) to challenge Prior to explain how his system avoids a form of the liar paradox. Drawing on observations in a review of Koyré (1946) by Church (1946), Prior (1958b) develops a more explicit deductive account of a propositionally quantified modal logic, and uses it to discuss the paradox. Prior (1961) continues this discussion; we return to it in the final Section 4.

Propositional quantifiers continue to play an important role in Prior's work after 1957, including the posthumously published Prior (1971). Especially noteworthy is the proposal to reduce possible worlds or instants of time to propositions in Prior (1967, p. 79). Prior (1968, pp. 205–207) develops this suggestion further, and formulates a number of related open problems in propositionally quantified modal logic. Very soon after this, Bull (1968, 1969), Kaplan (1970b), and Fine (1969, 1970) undertake systematic investigations of propositionally quantified modal logic. Model-theoretically, these discussions employ the famous possible worlds models of Kripke (1959, 1963a). In such models, propositional quantifiers can straightforwardly be evaluated by letting them range over sets of worlds in a given model; in fact, such an interpretation of propositional quantifiers is already discussed by Kripke (1959, pp. 12–13).

Propositional quantifiers can also be found in a number of philosophical applications in this period. An important example arises from a resurgence of interest in Ramsey's deflationism about truth; see, for example, Sellars (1960) and Heidelberger (1968). (While Sellars does not refer to Ramsey, he mentions

Carnap (1942), who in turn cites Ramsey (1923). It is also worth noting that Sellars is likely to have been familiar with propositional quantification in modal logic, since, as noted by deVries (2020), he studied modal logic with Langford around the time of publication of the first edition of Lewis and Langford (1959 [1932]).) Combined with a defense of propositional quantifiers by Grover (1970, 1972), this leads to a version of the deflationary theory of truth called the *prosentential theory of truth* by Grover et al. (1975). For further examples of uses of propositional quantifiers in this period, see Fitch (1963).

In a few short years, from 1967 to 1970, an immense amount of progress is made on propositionally quantified modal logic. Many of the most fundamental results in the area are established in this period, which will be covered in detail later, with references to the original publications. The outstanding achievement in this period is an article of Fine (1970), which focuses on propositionally quantified modal logic interpreted over possible worlds models. It is hard to convey a sense of just how many important contributions are contained in the eleven short pages of this article, including axiomatizations, model constructions, and results on completeness, decidability, and the failure of recursive axiomatizability. The multitude of references to it in this Element will give something of an impression of its importance. However, as a consequence of the wealth of results in this short article, proofs are often only sketched in the barest outlines.

Later Developments (1975–present) After an explosion of work on propositional quantifiers around the year 1970, interest in the topic seems to drop as rapidly as it arose. Two reasons may contribute to the waning of propositional quantifiers at this point: First, Arthur Prior, the chief proponent of propositional quantifiers in the 1960s, dies in 1969. Second, Quine (1986 [1970]) argues influentially against both modal and higher-order logic (where propositional quantifiers count as an instance of the latter). From a Quinean standpoint, modal logic with propositional quantifiers manages to combine two conceptual confusions in one very simple package.

Whatever the reasons for the lack of interest in propositional quantifiers in modal logic, little work is done in the field for roughly the next twenty years. This changes from the mid 1990s, as illustrated by publications of Ghilardi and Zawadowski (1995), Kaminski and Tiomkin (1996), Kremer (1997c), Antonelli and Thomason (2002) and ten Cate (2006). Especially in the last decade, one finds a marked resurgence of higher-order modal logic in philosophy, in no small part due to the influence of Williamson (2013). A number of interesting philosophical arguments require propositional quantifiers but no other higher-order quantifiers, and can therefore naturally be formulated in propositionally quantified modal logic. For examples in this Element, see the discussion of the knowability paradox in Section 2.3, the reduction of possible worlds to propositions in Section 2.5, the contingency of propositional existence in Section 3.6, and the paradox of Epimenides in Section 4.

Over the last 60 years, many important results on propositionally quantified modal logics are obtained, and many interesting applications are discussed. Some examples of applications will be discussed in what follows, involving epistemic and alethic modalities. Propositional quantifiers are also used in the context of applications involving other modalities, such as deontic (see Prior (1958a), Lokhorst (2006) and Rönnedal (2020)) and temporal (see Kesten and Pnueli (2002) and French and Reynolds (2003)).

In these respects, propositionally quantified modal logic resembles standard propositional modal logic. However, due to periods of neglect, the propositionally quantified case is comparatively understudied, and especially lacking in general and systematic results. This is illustrated by the fact that a completeness theorem for the most straightforward algebraic model theory of the most straightforward propositionally quantified modal logic is only established very recently, by Holliday (2019). The field is rife with similar longstanding open questions, which are open not because of intrinsic mathematical difficulty, but because of a lack of interest. In order to encourage research on these questions, I will highlight some of them in the following sections.

Nonclassical Logics The preceding historical overview only covers propositional quantifiers in *modal* logic, as well as motivating philosophical discussions. As noted in Section 1.5, it therefore omits the other important context in which propositional quantifiers have been discussed, which is the study of nonclassical logics. Since nonclassical logics are beyond the scope of this Element, I won't attempt to trace the relevant developments in any detail. But for the benefit of the reader who wants to delve into propositional quantifiers in nonclassical logics, I list some relevant publications here.

For propositional quantifiers in intuitionistic logic, see Myhill (1953), Prawitz (1965, pp. 67–68), Gabbay (1974), Löb (1976), Sobolev (1977), Kreisel (1981), Troelstra (1981), Pitts (1992), Połacik (1993, 1998a,b), Skvortsov (1997), Kremer (1997b, 2018), Zach (2004), Ferreira (2006), Baaz and Preining (2008), Zdanowski (2009), and Sørensen and Urzyczyn (2010).

For propositional quantifiers in relevant logic, see Anderson and Belnap, Jr (1961), Anderson (1972), Routley and Meyer (1973, sect. 13–16), Anderson et al. (1992, ch. VI), Kremer (1993), Kremer (1997a), Goldblatt and Kane (2010), and Badia (2019).

There appear to be few investigations of propositional quantifiers in nonclassical settings apart from intuitionistic and relevant logics, although see Baaz and Veith (2000) and Baaz et al. (2000) for exceptions.

2 Relational Frames

2.1 Propositionally Quantified Modal Languages

We start with a formal definition of a language of propositionally quantified modal logic. There are a number of choice of points in setting up this definition.

First, it is clear that the language will have to be based on a choice of atomic proposition letters. Such letters could be divided into nonlogical constants and variables, but we won't need such a division: in all the applications discussed in this section, the role of nonlogical constants can be played by free variables. So we start from a countably infinite set of variables Φ. For elements of Φ, we use lowercase Roman letters, in particular p, q, and r, and the results of adding various indices to these letters.

Second, different choices of Boolean connectives may be included. Propositional modal logics are often defined using some small functionally complete set of connectives, that is, a set of connectives such that every polyadic function on truth-values is expressed by some complex formula. This is because the modal logics of interest typically do not distinguish between formulas which are equivalent by the principles of classical propositional logic. For example, if a modal logic does not distinguish between formulas of the form $\neg\varphi$ and $\varphi \to \bot$ in any context, then there is no reason to include $\neg$ as a connective of the language in addition to $\to$ and $\bot$; instead, we can simply introduce "$\neg\varphi$" as a way of abbreviating "$\varphi \to \bot$". The main reason for limiting the number of Boolean connectives is that it simplifies many definitions and proofs, and we follow this common practice here, using just $\to$ and $\bot$ as Boolean connectives. For concreteness, we use other Boolean connectives as abbreviations, as follows:

$$\neg\varphi := \varphi \to \bot$$
$$\varphi \lor \psi := \neg\varphi \to \psi$$
$$\varphi \land \psi := \neg(\varphi \to \neg\psi)$$
$$\varphi \leftrightarrow \psi := (\varphi \to \psi) \land (\psi \to \varphi)$$
$$\top := \neg\bot$$

The choice of $\to$ and $\bot$ may seem a strange one, since $\bot$ is not an especially natural connective; in particular, there is no obvious way of rendering it in English. From the perspective of translating the formal language into English, it would be more natural to start with, for example, $\neg$ and $\land$, which are very naturally read as "not" and "and". But $\to$ and $\bot$ have two formal advantages: $\to$ is the most important connective for stating standard axiomatic principles, so including it allows us to avoid using defined connectives in the statement of these principles. And various arguments are simplified by ensuring that $\top$ and $\bot$ contain no free variables (or quantifiers), which motivates including $\bot$ as primitive. It is worth noting that in the general context of classical modal logics as introduced in the next section, the choice of primitive Boolean connectives can make a substantial difference; see Makinson (1973) and Segerberg (1982) for discussion.

Quantifiers present a choice-point similar to that of Boolean connectives. In many logics, the existential and universal quantifiers are treated as each other's duals, so that, for example, formulas of the form $\exists p\varphi$ and $\neg\forall p\neg\varphi$ are not distinguished in any context. We take the universal quantifier $\forall$ as primitive, and introduce the existential quantifier as the following abbreviation:

$$\exists p\varphi := \neg\forall p\neg\varphi$$

It is worth noting that the definition of $\bot$ as $\forall pp$ discussed in Section 1.6 would be available to us for much of the following. However, we still include $\bot$ as a primitive connective, for two reasons: First, as noted, it can be helpful for $\top$ and $\bot$ to contain neither free variables nor quantifiers. Second, in discussing standard (i.e., quantifier-free) propositional modal logics, we still need to ensure that the set of Boolean connectives is functionally complete.

Finally, our languages will contain modal operators. Most discussions of modal logics only consider including a single unary operator $\Box$. But from the perspective of applications, *unary unimodal* logics are very limiting, as urged already by Scott (1970). First, many natural applications require multiple modal operators. For example, already the simple claim that every truth can be known requires two modal operators. Second, many natural modal connectives are polyadic, such as the (binary) counterfactual conditional $\Box\!\!\to$; see Lewis (1973). We therefore set up our formal language relative to a choice of operators, which we call a *modal signature*. This will be specified by a set O of modal operators, and a function ρ mapping every one of them to its arity. For example, a language containing a unary (necessity) operator $\Box$ and a binary (counterfactual) connective $\Box\!\!\to$ will be specified using the modal signature $\langle\{\Box,\Box\!\!\to\},\rho\rangle$, where $\rho(\Box) = 1$ and $\rho(\Box\!\!\to) = 2$.

All of these choices lead us to the following definition:

Definition 2.1.1 *A* modal signature *is a pair* $\sigma = \langle O,\rho\rangle$, *where O is a set, and* $\rho : O \to \mathbb{N}$.

Let Φ be a countably infinite set of propositional variables. Given a modal signature $\sigma = \langle O, \rho \rangle$, $\mathcal{L}^\sigma$ is the smallest set such that:

(i)   If $p \in \Phi$, then $p \in \mathcal{L}^\sigma$.
(ii) $\bot \in \mathcal{L}^\sigma$.
(iii) If $\varphi, \psi \in \mathcal{L}^\sigma$, then $(\varphi \to \psi) \in \mathcal{L}^\sigma$.
(iv) If $o \in O$ and $\varphi_1, \ldots, \varphi_{\rho(o)} \in \mathcal{L}^\sigma$, then $o\varphi_1 \ldots \varphi_{\rho(o)} \in \mathcal{L}^\sigma$.
(v)   If $p \in \Phi$ and $\varphi \in \mathcal{L}^\sigma$, then $\forall p \varphi \in \mathcal{L}^\sigma$.

$\mathcal{L}^\sigma_{\mathrm{qf}}$ is the set of quantifier-free formulas of $\mathcal{L}^\sigma$, that is, the smallest set satisfying conditions (i)–(iv) for $\mathcal{L}^\sigma_{\mathrm{qf}}$ instead of $\mathcal{L}^\sigma$.

A few clarifications and remarks on this definition are in order:

First, the letter "p" is not itself assumed to be a propositional variable (i.e., a member of Φ); rather, it is used as a variable in the metalanguage (mathematical English) to stand for a member of Φ. Nevertheless, we will use such letters later to specify particular formulas, such as $\Box(p \to q) \to (\Box p \to \Box q)$. The intention in such uses is that p and q are distinct members of Φ; since it won't matter which elements are chosen, they are not further specified.

Second, lowercase Greek letters like "φ" and "ψ" are used as metalinguistic variables ranging over formulas. In clauses (i)–(v), concatenation is indicated using juxtaposition. To illustrate this, consider clause (iii): Using "φ" and "ψ" as metalanguage variables over formulas (i.e., elements) of $\mathcal{L}^\sigma$, "$(\varphi \to \psi)$" is used to denote the result of concatenating (, φ, $\to$, ψ, and). Strictly speaking, we have not said what (, $\to$, and) are. But since it does not matter, as long as they are pairwise distinct – just as it does not matter exactly what the elements of Φ are – we will leave this unspecified.

Third, according to clause (iv), a formula obtained using an application of a binary modal operator o has the form $o\varphi\psi$. However, some modal operators, such as $\Box\!\!\to$, are more commonly used infix rather than prefix: it is more common to write $(\varphi \mathbin{\Box\!\!\to} \psi)$ rather than $\Box\!\!\to\varphi\psi$. We therefore allow the former notation as an abbreviation for the latter formula. When not required to resolve any structural ambiguities, we drop the parentheses, as we do for $\to$. Among binary operators, we assume that $\wedge$ and $\vee$ bind stronger than any other. So, to illustrate, we write $p \to q \wedge r$ to abbreviate $(p \to (q \wedge r))$.

Finally, the notion of a free occurrence of a variable is defined as usual: an occurrence of p is *bound* if it is in the scope of a quantifier $\forall p$, and *free* otherwise. A variable p is *free in* φ if there is a free occurrence of p in φ. A formula ψ is *free for p in φ* if no free occurrence of a variable in ψ becomes bound when every free occurrence of p in φ is replaced by ψ. If ψ is free for p in φ, we write $\varphi[\psi/p]$ for the result of this replacement. We generalize this last notation to finite sequences, writing $\varphi[\psi_1/p_1, \ldots, \psi_n/p_n]$ for the result of simultaneously replacing every free occurrence of p_i in φ by ψ_i, assuming ψ_i is free for p_i in φ (for $1 \leq i \leq n$, with $p_1, \ldots, p_n$ being pairwise distinct).

2.2 Modal Logics Based on Classical Logic

Having defined the languages of propositionally quantified modal logics, we turn to the logics themselves. As common in modal logic, we will think of a logic primarily as a set of formulas. Such a set will be required to satisfy certain closure conditions, which correspond to axioms or rules in a Hilbert calculus. Other proof-theoretic approaches are possible, but we won't consider them here. For examples involving propositional quantifiers, see the tableaux systems of Kripke (1959), Bull (1969), Rönnedal (2019, 2020) and Blackburn et al. (2020), and the (labeled) natural deduction system of Pascucci (2019).

The conditions on logics which we will assume for the most part ensure the derivability of any principle of classical propositional logic and any principle of elementary quantification theory for propositional quantifiers. There are many different ways of imposing this requirement. We proceed as follows: First, we demand that every *tautology* is included. Tautologies are the formulas involving only propositional variables and Boolean connectives which are true under every truth-value assignment; by the soundness and completeness of classical propositional logic, they are also just the theorems of classical propositional logic. Second, we demand that the relevant set is closed under the rule of *modus ponens*. With this rule, we could modify the first condition, and require only a finite set of axioms to be included from which all tautologies are derivable using modus ponens. This choice points won't matter in the following, so we simply include all tautologies; note that the definition of being a tautology using truthtables constitutes a decision procedure. Turning to quantifiers, we require the inclusion of every instance of *universal instantiation*. This condition encapsulates the idea that if a given condition holds for every proposition, then it holds as well for the proposition expressed by any given formula ψ. Finally, we require closure under *universal generalization*: If a conditional $\varphi \rightarrow \psi$ is contained in the set and p is not free in φ, then $\varphi \rightarrow \forall p \psi$ must be contained as well. This condition encapsulates the idea that propositional variables stand for arbitrary propositions, and the thought that if a condition ψ is guaranteed to hold for an *arbitrary* p (on the assumption of φ), then it must hold for *every* p (assuming φ). These four conditions suffice to ensure that the basic principles of classical logic are included. We therefore call the relevant logics *classical*:

Definition 2.2.1 *Given any modal signature σ, define the following conditions on a set* $\Lambda \subseteq \mathcal{L}^\sigma$:

(Taut) $\varphi \in \Lambda$ *whenever* φ *is a tautology.*
(MP) *If* $\varphi \in \Lambda$ *and* $\varphi \rightarrow \psi \in \Lambda$, *then* $\psi \in \Lambda$.
(UI) $\forall p \varphi \rightarrow \varphi[\psi/p] \in \Lambda$ *whenever* ψ *is free for p in* φ.
(UG) *If* $\varphi \rightarrow \psi \in \Lambda$ *and p is not free in* φ, *then* $\varphi \rightarrow \forall p \psi \in \Lambda$.

A classical propositionally quantified modal logic *is a set* Λ *which satisfies all four of these conditions.*

Strictly speaking, the notion of a classical propositionally quantified modal logic is relative to the signature σ, but since the signature will usually be clear from context, we don't usually mention this explicitly. In the literature, the notion of a classical propositionally quantified modal logic is rarely isolated. Instead, stronger conditions are usually imposed, along lines which we will discuss below. For an exception in the unary unimodal case, see Ding (2018, p. 220), who uses the label "Π-logic".

From the four constraints of classical propositionally quantified modal logics, we can show that any such logic contains all of the familiar principles of elementary quantification theory for propositional quantifiers. We can also show that any such logic is closed under *uniform substitution*: any free propositional variable may be replaced by any formula free for it in the relevant context. The following result gives some examples of such quantificational principles, including those used in the axiomatic system of Fine (1970).

Proposition 2.2.2 *If* Λ *is a classical propositionally quantified modal logic, then it satisfies all of the following conditions:*

(1) If φ *is a tautology, then* $\varphi[\psi/p] \in \Lambda$.
(2) If $\varphi \in \Lambda$, *then* $\forall p \varphi \in \Lambda$.
(3) If $\varphi \in \Lambda$ *and* ψ *is free for p in* φ, *then* $\varphi[\psi/p] \in \Lambda$.
(4) $\varphi \rightarrow \forall p \varphi \in \Lambda$, *whenever p is not free in* φ.
(5) $\forall p(\varphi \rightarrow \psi) \rightarrow (\forall p \varphi \rightarrow \forall p \psi) \in \Lambda$.
(6) $\varphi[\psi/p] \rightarrow \exists p \varphi \in \Lambda$, *whenever* ψ *is free for p in* φ.
(7) $\forall p \varphi \leftrightarrow \forall q(\varphi[q/p]) \in \Lambda$, *whenever q is free for p in* φ.

Proof We consider the first three items; the rest can be deduced from these by standard arguments.

(1): Assume φ is a tautology. Then so is $\top \rightarrow \varphi$, which is therefore a member of Λ, by Taut. So with UG, $\top \rightarrow \forall p \varphi \in \Lambda$. As $\top \in \Lambda$ by Taut, $\forall p \varphi \in \Lambda$

follows with MP. By UI, $\forall p\varphi \rightarrow \varphi[\psi/p] \in \Lambda$. ($\psi$ must be free for p in φ, as φ is quantifier-free.) So by MP, $\varphi[\psi/p] \in \Lambda$.

(2): Assume $\varphi \in \Lambda$. Since $p \rightarrow (\top \rightarrow p)$ is a tautology, it follows with (1) that $\varphi \rightarrow (\top \rightarrow \varphi) \in \Lambda$. So $\top \rightarrow \varphi \in \Lambda$ by MP, whence $\top \rightarrow \forall p\varphi \in \Lambda$ by UG. Since $\top$ is a tautology, it follows with Taut and MP that $\forall p\varphi \in \Lambda$.

(3): Assume that $\varphi \in \Lambda$ and ψ is free for p in φ. Then $\forall p\varphi \in \Lambda$ by (2). By UI, $\forall p\varphi \rightarrow \varphi[\psi/p] \in \Lambda$, and so $\varphi[\psi/p] \in \Lambda$ with MP. $\square$

As a special case of (3), we obtain the observation that relabeling free variables does not affect membership in a classical propositionally quantified modal logic Λ: if Λ contains φ, then Λ also contains $\varphi[q/p]$, as long as q is free for p in φ. Further, from (7) we can see the equivalence of a universally quantified statements with the result of relabeling the bound variable of the outermost quantifier. By a straightforward induction, this can be extended to relabeling the bound variables of any quantifiers which are not in the scope of any modal operators. But we cannot remove the restriction on modal operators, since we are not assuming that formulas which are equivalent by the lights of Λ are interchangeable within modal operators. This is intentional: At this point, we don't want to impose any limitations on the distinctions which can be drawn by modal operators. For example, we will consider a binary operator of identity $=$ in Section 4. We don't want to assume at this point that, for example, $(\forall pp) = (\forall qq)$, even if it is plausible. Consequently, we cannot assume that bound variables can always be relabeled. It is therefore important that such a relabeling is not built into the definition of $\varphi[\psi/p]$, as it sometimes is, for example, by Bull (1969, pp. 257–258). In many kinds of propositionally quantified modal logics (in particular normal and congruential ones, defined later), bound variables *can* be relabeled, but this must be established on the basis of the particular constraints on modal operators.

Having defined the notion of a classical propositionally quantified modal logic, it will be useful to define a corresponding notion for the quantifier-free case. For our purposes, it will be useful not just to consider sets of quantifier-free formulas satisfying Taut and MP, but sets which are also closed under *uniform substitution*: Since a given proposition letter p stands for an arbitrary proposition, a formula φ should only be contained in a logic if $\varphi[\psi/p]$ is contained as well. There was no need to impose this requirement in the presence of quantifiers, as shown by Proposition 2.2.2. Without quantifiers, this natural condition must be imposed separately:

Definition 2.2.3 *Given any modal signature σ, a* classical modal logic *is a set $\Lambda \subseteq \mathcal{L}^\sigma_{\text{qf}}$ which satisfies* Taut, MP, *and the following condition:*

(US) *If $\varphi \in \Lambda$, $p \in \Phi$, and $\psi \in \mathcal{L}^{\sigma}_{\mathrm{qf}}$, then $\varphi[\psi/p] \in \Lambda$.*

The terminology used here comes apart somewhat from established terminology, which uses the label "modal logic" for what we are calling a "classical modal logic"; see, for example, Segerberg (1971, p. 8). Segerberg also uses the label "classical modal logic" for a different notion, which we call "congruential modal logic" in Section 3.1, following Makinson (1973, p. 196). The reason for our use of "classical" for the notion just defined is that it corresponds to the previous notion of classicality in the propositionally quantified case. As noted, there are modal logics based on non-classical propositional logics, and in Section 3.5, we will see logics which weaken the principles associated with the quantifiers. Because of these reasons, we require the qualifier "classical".

So far, we have taken an abstract approach to modal logics as sets of formulas satisfying certain closure conditions. One might wonder why we haven't considered any proof systems. In fact, each closure condition considered here corresponds to a schematic axiom or rule, and a constraint like classicality can be turned into a proof-theoretic concept. I will illustrate the point using the notion of a classical propositionally quantified modal logic, but it is easy to see that it applies as well to classical modal logics and similar concepts defined below.

First, we note that for every set of formulas $\Gamma \subseteq \mathcal{L}^{\sigma}$, there is a unique smallest classical propositionally quantified modal logic including Γ, namely the intersection of all classical propositionally quantified modal logics including Γ. This intersection is guaranteed to be well-defined, since $\mathcal{L}^{\sigma}$ trivially includes Γ and satisfies the four closure conditions. The smallest classical propositionally quantified modal logic including Γ can alternatively be characterized as the set of theorems of the proof system which contains as axioms the tautologies and instances of the schema of universal instantiation (as in Taut and UI), as well as the elements of Γ, and as rules modus ponens and universal generalization (as in MP and UG). We therefore define:

Definition 2.2.4 *For any set $\Gamma \subseteq \mathcal{L}^{\sigma}_{\mathrm{qf}}$, the classical modal logic axiomatized by Γ, written $\mathrm{C}^{\sigma}\Gamma$, is the smallest classical modal logic including Γ. For any set $\Gamma \subseteq \mathcal{L}^{\sigma}$, the classical propositionally quantified modal logic axiomatized by Γ, written $\mathrm{C}^{\sigma}_{\Pi}\Gamma$, is the smallest classical propositionally quantified modal logic including Γ.*

If Γ is a finite set $\{\gamma_1, \ldots, \gamma_n\}$, we also write $\mathrm{C}^{\sigma}_{(\Pi)}\gamma_1 \ldots \gamma_n$ instead of $\mathrm{C}^{\sigma}_{(\Pi)}\Gamma$. In particular, $\mathrm{C}^{\sigma}_{(\Pi)}$ is the smallest classical (propositionally quantified) modal logic. For brevity, we usually omit mention of the modal signature σ in C^{σ}, unless it is not clear from context. All of these conventions will be applied to analogs of this definition for normal and congruential modal logics as well.

A set of formulas is a classical propositionally quantified modal logic if and only if it is the classical propositionally quantified modal logic axiomatized by Γ, for some set Γ. This observation gives us a deductive formulation of classical propositionally quantified modal logics. It also follows that every classical propositionally quantified modal logic Λ is axiomatized by *some* set, in particular by Λ itself, so in this sense, every such logic is axiomatizable. In this sense, being axiomatizable is an uninteresting notion. In later discussions of axiomatizability, we will therefore consider a more demanding notion. If we think of a logic (set of formulas) Λ as given axiomatically, we say that φ is a *theorem* of, or *derivable* in, Λ if $\varphi \in \Lambda$.

2.3 Relational Frames and Normality

The remainder of this section focuses on the most well-known model theory for modal languages: the relational frames of Kripke (1963a). Such relational frames can be defined for a language of any modal signature, as it is done by Blackburn et al. (2001, p. 20), but they are especially natural in the case of unary modal operators. In Section 3.1, we consider a generalization of relational frames which extends straightforwardly to polyadic modal operators. For the remainder of this section, we only consider unary modal signatures, where a signature $\langle O, \rho \rangle$ is *unary* just in case ρ maps every element of O to 1. In this case, we omit mention of ρ and simply write $\mathcal{L}^O$. If O is a finite set $\{\Box_1, \ldots, \Box_n\}$, we abbreviate this further to $\mathcal{L}^{\Box_1 \cdots \Box_n}$ (and correspondingly in analogous contexts that follow). Analogous to the definition of $\exists$ as the dual of $\forall$, we introduce the following abbreviation for the dual of $\Box$:

$$\Diamond\varphi := \neg\Box\neg\varphi$$

This convention is extended in the obvious way to $\Box_1$ and $\Diamond_1$, and so on. Depending on the interpretation of $\Box$, there is often a corresponding natural interpretation of $\Diamond$. For example, in contexts in which $\Box$ is interpreted as a notion of necessity, $\Diamond$ can usually be interpreted as the corresponding notion of possibility.

Kripke's definition of relational frames combines two ideas: First, a relational frame is based on a set of *(possible) worlds* or *points*, each of which settles the truth-value of every formula. (This notion of truth is relative to an interpretation of the atomic proposition letters – we consider this in a moment.) Second, for every (unary) modal operator $\Box$, a relational frame contains a binary relation of *accessibility* $R_\Box$ among worlds which determines the interpretation of $\square$, where $\square\varphi$ is true in a world just in case φ is true in every accessible world. It is worth noting already at this point that these two ideas are separable: Section 3.1 will discuss a class of models which are based on worlds but not accessibility relations, and Section 3.2 will mention a class of models in which the interpretation of modal operators involves accessibility relations, but no worlds.

The interpretation of formulas in relational frames is relative to a function which maps every proposition letter to the set of worlds in which it is true. Since proposition letters are often considered as constants, such a function is often called a *valuation function*; when a frame is enriched with such a function it is often called a *model*. Here we conceive of proposition letters as variables, so we call such a function an *assignment function* instead. With this, the interpretation of propositional quantifiers at a world is straightforward: $\forall p\varphi$ is true relative to an assignment function a just in case φ is true relative to every assignment function which agrees with a on every propositional variable with the possible exception of p. This interpretation can already be found in Kripke (1959). An alternative approach restricts the admissible assignment functions, allowing only certain sets of worlds to serve as the interpretation of a propositional variable; we return to this in Section 3.5.

To state the truth-conditions of universal and modal formulas, we introduce the following conventions: $a[x/p]$ is the function mapping p to x and every propositional variable $q \neq p$ to $a(q)$. (Note that this convention is distinct from the convention of writing $\varphi[\psi/p]$ for the result of replacing every free occurrence of p in φ by ψ.) $R(w)$ is the set of elements v such that Rwv; for any set x, $R[x]$ is the set of elements v such that Rwv for some $w \in x$. We can now define relational frames formally as follows:

Definition 2.3.1 *A relational frame (for a unary modal signature O) is a structure* $\mathfrak{F} = \langle W, R_\square \rangle_{\square \in O}$ *such that W is a set and $R_\square \subseteq W \times W$ for every $\square \in O$. An assignment function (for $\mathfrak{F}$) is a function $a \colon \Phi \to \mathcal{P}(W)$. A formula $\varphi \in \mathcal{L}^O$ being* true *relative to $\mathfrak{F}$, $w \in W$, and a, written $\mathfrak{F}, w, a \Vdash \varphi$, is defined by the following recursive clauses:*

$\mathfrak{F}, w, a \Vdash p$ *if and only if $w \in a(p)$*

$\mathfrak{F}, w, a \nVdash \bot$

$\mathfrak{F}, w, a \Vdash \varphi \to \psi$ *if and only if $\mathfrak{F}, w, a \Vdash \varphi$ only if $\mathfrak{F}, w, a \Vdash \psi$*

$\mathfrak{F}, w, a \Vdash \forall p\varphi$ *if and only if $\mathfrak{F}, w, a[x/p] \Vdash \varphi$ for all $x \subseteq W$*

$\mathfrak{F}, w, a \Vdash \square\varphi$ *if and only if $\mathfrak{F}, v, a \Vdash \varphi$ for all $v \in R_\square(w)$*

From this, two notions of validity *are derived, letting C be a class of relational frames:*

$\mathfrak{F} \Vdash \varphi$ *if* $\mathfrak{F}, w, a \Vdash \varphi$ *for all* $w \in W$ *and* $a \colon \Phi \to \mathcal{P}(W)$

$C \Vdash \varphi$ *if* $\mathfrak{F} \Vdash \varphi$ *for all* $\mathfrak{F}$ *in* C

Relational frames provide a very flexible model theory for modal languages: Every class of relational frames C determines a logic, namely the set of formulas valid on every frame in C. For example, in order to ensure the validity of the principle $\Box p \to p$, we may focus on relational frames in which $R_\Box$ is reflexive, and to ensure the validity of the principle $\exists p(\Box p \land \neg p)$, we may focus on relational frames in which $R_\Box$ is irreflexive. This is a general feature of model theories for modal languages, so we define generally:

Definition 2.3.2 *If* Γ *is a set of formulas and* C *is a class of structures such that a relation of validity* $\Vdash$ *has been defined between members of the two classes,* $\Gamma(C)$ *is the set of formulas* $\gamma \in \Gamma$ *such that* $\mathfrak{S} \Vdash \gamma$ *for all structures* $\mathfrak{S}$ *in* C.

We call $\mathcal{L}^\sigma(C)$ the *propositionally quantified modal logic of* C, and $\mathcal{L}^\sigma_{qf}(C)$ the *modal logic of* C. We can show that the (propositionally quantified) modal logic of any class of relational frames is a classical (propositionally quantified) modal logic. In fact, the logics of classes of relational frames are guaranteed to satisfy two additional conditions, which lead to the following notion of normality:

Definition 2.3.3 *For any set* $\Lambda \subseteq \mathcal{L}^O$, *we define the following conditions:*

(K) $\Box(p \to q) \to (\Box p \to \Box q) \in \Lambda$, *for all* $\Box \in O$.

(Nec) *If* $\varphi \in \Lambda$ *and* $\Box \in O$, *then* $\Box\varphi \in \Lambda$.

Λ *is a* normal (propositionally quantified) modal logic *if it is a classical (propositionally quantified) modal logic satisfying* K *and* Nec.

Since normality plays a central role in the remainder of this section, we abbreviate "normal (propositionally quantified) modal logic" as "NML" ("NPQML"). It is a standard result in modal logic that the modal logic of any class of relational frames is normal. As the next proposition notes, this extends to the propositionally quantified case:

Proposition 2.3.4 *For any class* C *of relational frames,* $\mathcal{L}^O(C)$ *is an* NPQML.

Proof It is routine to show that $\mathcal{L}^O(C)$ satisfies each of the six conditions. □

It is worth noting that in contrast to the notion of classicality, normality is not motivated independently of the model theory of relational frames. This is illustrated by the fact that in the early literature on modal logic, at least two other notions of normality were employed; see McKinsey and Tarski (1948, p. 7),

Kripke (1963a, p. 67), and Lemmon (1977 [1966], p. 30). It is only in systematic explorations of relational frame semantics, such as Makinson (1966, p. 379) and Segerberg (1971, p. 12), that the now-common notion of normality emerged (initially called "semi-normality" by Makinson). In the literature on propositionally quantified modal logics, a definition of normality for the unimodal case can be found in Ding (2018, 2021a) and Holliday (2019).

Analogous to the case of classicality, normality gives rise to a notion of normal logics axiomatized by a given set of axioms:

Definition 2.3.5 *For any set* $\Gamma \subseteq \mathcal{L}_{\text{qf}}^O$, *the* NML *axiomatized by* Γ, *written* $K^O\Gamma$, *is the smallest* NML *including* Γ. *For any set* $\Gamma \subseteq \mathcal{L}^O$, *the* NPQML *axiomatized by* Γ, *written* $K_\Pi^O\Gamma$, *is the smallest* NPQML *including* Γ.

Just as a class of relational frames determines a set of formulas (the set of formulas valid on the class), a set of formulas determines a class of relational frames: the class of relational frames on which every member of the set is valid. Again, this idea extends to any language and class of structures among which a notion of validity has been defined:

Definition 2.3.6 *If* Γ *is a set of formulas and* C *is a class of structures such that a relation of validity* $\Vdash$ *has been defined between members of the two classes, then* C(Γ) *is the class of structures* $\mathfrak{S}$ *in* C *such that* $\mathfrak{S} \Vdash \gamma$ *for all* $\gamma \in \Gamma$.

We write R for the class of all relational frames (for a given modal signature), and say that R(Γ) is the class of relational frames *defined by* Γ. Since every NML defines a class of relational frames, and every class of relational frames gives rise to an NPQML, we obtain a model-theoretic way of extending NMLs by propositional quantifiers: Given an NML Λ, we may consider the NPQML of validities on the class of frames validating Λ, namely, $\mathcal{L}^O(R(\Lambda))$. Adapting notation of Fine (1970), we introduce the following abbreviation (with O determined by context):

Definition 2.3.7 *If* Λ *is an* NML, *then* $\Lambda\pi+$ *is* $\mathcal{L}^O(R(\Lambda))$.

At this point, it is worth mentioning two other notations for propositionally quantified modal logics used in the literature: First, Fine (1970) introduces the notation $\Lambda\pi$ alongside $\Lambda\pi+$, defined in terms of a wider class of models. We return to this notation in Section 3.5, when we consider the relevant models. Second, Bull (1969) defines, for a propositional modal *proof system* S, a proof system SΠ obtained by adding rules corresponding to UI and UG. Recent authors including Ding (2018) and Holliday (2019) have adapted this notation to propositional modal *logics* Λ; they write $\Lambda\Pi$ for the smallest NPQML including Λ. On this notation, K$\Gamma\Pi$ is what we here write K$_\Pi\Gamma$. The reason why

I don't follow this notation here is the following: Given an NML Λ, there are several ways of adding propositional quantifiers. For example, we might consider the smallest classical propositionally quantified modal logic including Λ, or the smallest NPQML including Λ. Adding Π as a subscript to K makes clear that the normal extension is intended. The downside of this notation is that it makes it awkward to specify normal propositionally quantified extensions when the relevant NML is not given in the form KΓ. The most prominent cases are the Lewis systems S4 and S5. This awkwardness can be mitigated by introducing the convention of writing $S_\Pi 4$ and $S_\Pi 5$ instead of $K_\Pi S4$ and $K_\Pi S5$, respectively, and analogously for their extensions. Similarly, some NMLs have names of the form KX, without X being an axiom or list of axioms; an example is K3, which we discuss in Section 2.6. In these cases, we also write $K_\Pi X$ for $K_\Pi KX$.

Classes of relational frames, normal modal logics, and the relation of validity give rise to many questions which have been central to the study of modal logic. Such questions are often phrased in terms of soundness and completeness: A normal modal logic Λ is said to be *sound* with respect to a class of relational frames C if every member of Λ is valid on C, and *complete* if every formula valid on C is a member of Λ. Establishing these properties is especially interesting if Λ is specified as KΓ, for a finite set of axioms Γ.

For every class of relational frames C, there is a unique normal modal logic which is sound and complete with respect to it, namely $\mathcal{L}_{\mathrm{qf}}^O(\mathrm{C})$; this is the logic *determined by* C. But conversely, it is not obvious that every normal modal logic KΓ is sound and complete with respect to some class of frames. If it is, then it is sound and complete in particular with respect to R(Γ), and so KΓ = $\mathcal{L}_{\mathrm{qf}}^O(\mathrm{R}(\Gamma))$. K$\Gamma$ is always sound with respect to R(Γ), but it is not obvious that KΓ should always be complete with respect to R(Γ). That is, it may be that some formula φ is *valid* on every relational frame in the class defined by Γ, even though φ cannot be *derived* from Γ, in the sense that $\varphi \notin$ KΓ. In fact, Thomason (1974) and Fine (1974) showed that there are normal modal logics which are not determined by any class of relational frames. Such logics are often called *Kripke-incomplete*.

Although not every normal modal logic is Kripke-complete, very many natural normal modal logics are so. This includes every normal unimodal logic axiomatized by a subset of the following common modal axioms:

D $\quad \Box p \rightarrow \Diamond p$

T $\quad \Box p \rightarrow p$

B $\quad p \rightarrow \Box \Diamond p$

4 $\quad \Box p \rightarrow \Box \Box p$

5 $\quad \Diamond p \rightarrow \Box \Diamond p$

For example, KT is sound and complete with respect to the class of relational frames on which T is valid, which contains just those relational frames with a reflexive accessibility relation, and K is sound and complete with respect to the class of all relational frames.

Much of the remainder of this section will be concerned with these kinds of questions in the propositionally quantified modal case. As it turns out, in the presence of propositional quantifiers, the situation changes drastically: $K_\Pi\Gamma$ is incomplete with respect to $R(\Gamma)$ for very many natural choices of axioms Γ. This incompleteness can have a number of different sources, which we explore in the following.

Before turning to these model-theoretic questions in subsequent sections, it is worth noting a purely deductive question which appears not to have been considered in the literature. Say that a propositionally quantified modal logic Π is a *conservative extension* of a modal logic Λ if the quantifier-free theorems of Π are just the theorems of Λ; that is, if $\Pi \cap \mathcal{L}_{qf}^O = \Lambda$. One would not expect that adding propositional quantifiers governed by UI and UG to a given propositional modal logic would allow the derivation of any additional purely modal (i.e., quantifier-free) principles. And indeed, it is not very difficult to show the following, as I do in Fritz (unpublished):

Proposition 2.3.8 *For every quantifier-free set* Γ, $C_\Pi\Gamma$ *is a conservative extension of* $C\Gamma$.

However, there is a closely related question which is more difficult to settle. This is the analogous question for normal logics, namely the question whether $K_\Pi\Gamma$ is always a conservative extension of $K\Gamma$. Note that this is not settled by the previous result: if we let Δ be $K\Gamma$, then $C\Delta$ is $K\Gamma$, and so $C_\Pi K\Gamma$ is a conservative extension of $K\Gamma$. But it doesn't obviously follow that $K_\Pi\Gamma$ is a conservative extension of $K\Gamma$: $K_\Pi\Gamma$ does, but $C_\Pi K\Gamma$ does not obviously allow quantified axioms to be necessitated. It is easy to see that if $K\Gamma$ is the logic of a class of relational frames, this class will also validate $K_\Pi\Gamma$, whence $K_\Pi\Gamma$ is a conservative extension of $K\Gamma$. But, as I show in Fritz (unpublished), there are cases of Kripke-incomplete NMLs $K\Gamma$ in which the incompleteness can be demonstrated deductively with the addition of quantifiers:

Proposition 2.3.9 *For some quantifier-free set* Γ, $K_\Pi\Gamma$ *is a nonconservative extension of* $K\Gamma$.

To conclude this section, we illustrate the usefulness of proof systems for propositionally quantified modal logics in applications with an argument known the *knowability paradox*. Informally, this is an argument for the surprising conclusion that if every truth is knowable, then every truth is known. It was first published by Fitch (1963), but it is due to Church (2009 [1945]) who formulated it in a referee report for an earlier version of Fitch's article. Many detailed discussions of the argument can be found in an edited volume on the argument, Salerno (2009). Informally, the argument goes as follows:

> Reasoning contrapositively, assume that some truth p is not known. We argue that in this case, it is an unknowable truth that p is an unknown truth. The argument assumes that the following principles of knowledge hold necessarily: first, a conjunction is known only if the conjuncts are known, and second, only truths are known. We can then argue as follows: If it were known that p is an unknown truth, then, first, p would be known, and second, it would be known that p is unknown. From the second of these consequences, it follows that p is unknown, which contradicts the first consequence. So it is not possibly known that p is an unknown truth, even though p is an unknown truth. Therefore, there is an unknowable truth, namely that p is an unknown truth. Since p is arbitrary, we can conclude generally that if there is any unknown truth, then there is an unknowable truth. Contrapositively, if every truth is knowable, then every truth is known.

This argument is clearly sufficiently complicated for formalization to shed light on the inferential assumptions required to arrive at the conclusion. The argument is also very naturally formalized using propositional quantifiers. In fact, Church and Fitch employed propositional quantifiers in their original formulations of the argument. The most straightforward formalization uses two modal operators: a unary operator K for "it is known that" and a unary operator $\Box$ for "it is necessary that". Then the conclusion of the knowability paradox can straightforwardly be stated as follows:

(KNOWABILITY PARADOX) $\forall p(p \rightarrow \Diamond Kp) \rightarrow \forall p(p \rightarrow Kp)$

Even just regimenting the conclusion of this argument using propositional quantifiers is illuminating: although the informal statement and argument appealed to *truth*, no property of truth needs to invoked in the formal statement using propositional quantifiers. (For more on this point, see Section 1.6.) But the full potential of formalization is only realized once we regiment the informal argument as a deductive proof. From such a deduction, we can glean exactly which assumptions are needed to carry out the argument. It turns out that all that is required, in addition to the assumptions encoded in NPQMLS, is the axiom $Kp \rightarrow p$ which states that knowledge is factive:

Proposition 2.3.10 KNOWABILITY PARADOX *is provable in* $K_{\Pi}^{\Box K} Kp \rightarrow p$.

Proof By the following sketch of a derivation (eliding some details of straightforward inferences in which quantifiers are not involved):

$$
\begin{array}{lll}
(1) & K(p \wedge \neg Kp) \rightarrow (Kp \wedge K \neg Kp) & K^K \\
(2) & K \neg Kp \rightarrow \neg Kp & Kp \rightarrow p \\
(3) & \neg K(p \wedge \neg Kp) & 1, 2 \\
(4) & \Box \neg K(p \wedge \neg Kp) & 3, \text{Nec} \\
(5) & \forall p(p \rightarrow \Diamond Kp) \rightarrow ((p \wedge \neg Kp) \rightarrow \Diamond K(p \wedge \neg Kp)) & \text{UI} \\
(6) & \forall p(p \rightarrow \Diamond Kp) \rightarrow (p \rightarrow Kp) & 4, 5 \\
(7) & \forall p(p \rightarrow \Diamond Kp) \rightarrow \forall p(p \rightarrow Kp) & 6, \text{UG} \quad \Box
\end{array}
$$

2.4 The Barcan Formula and Atomicity

Returning to the sources of incompleteness of NPQMLS with respect to classes of relational frames, we begin with two relatively straightforward cases. They are two important schematic principles governing the interactions between modal operators and propositional quantifiers which are valid on all relational frames, but not guaranteed to be contained in NPQMLS.

The first principle is a propositional version of the *Barcan formula* of first-order modal logic, named after Barcan (1946). This is the following schema, where $\varphi \in \mathcal{L}^O$ and $\Box \in O$:

(Bc) $\forall p \Box \varphi \rightarrow \Box \forall p \varphi$

The status of this schematic principle in the propositionally quantified setting is analogous to its status in the setting of first-order modal logic: First, every instance of Bc is valid on every relational frame. This follows by the fact that propositional quantifiers range over the same domain at every world, namely the powerset $\mathcal{P}(W)$. Second, every instance of the converse of Bc, that is, the schema $\Box \forall p \varphi \rightarrow \forall p \Box \varphi$, is derivable in every NPQML. Third, for any modality $\Box$, the instances of Bc for $\Box$ are derivable in any NPQML which contains the modal principle B for $\Box$. The latter two of these claims, concerned with derivability, can be established by straightforward analogs of standard derivations in the first-order case, as found, for example, in Hughes and Cresswell (1996, pp. 245–247). Finally, some instances of Bc are *not* derivable in certain NPQMLS (not containing B for the relevant modality). This can be shown using models presented below, in Sections 3.1 and 3.6.

The second kind of principle arises from the fact that for every world w of a relational frame, the domain of propositions $\mathcal{P}(W)$ contains the singleton $\{w\}$. From an algebraic perspective, such propositions can be seen as *atomic* elements; we return to this perspective in Section 3.2. We therefore call singletons of worlds *atomic propositions*. Such propositions have special properties which can be expressed in a propositionally quantified language. This leads to a cluster of related principles which are valid on relational frames but which are not in general derivable in NPQMLs.

For the first such principle, note that for every world w, the atomic proposition $\{w\}$ is true in w and no other (accessible) world. Thus, at w, every true proposition q is strictly implied by $\{w\}$, in the sense that necessarily, if $\{w\}$ then q. Relational frames therefore validate the following schematic principle, which says that there is a proposition p with this feature (for any $\square \in O$):

(At) $\exists p(p \wedge \forall q(q \rightarrow \square(p \rightarrow q)))$

For another example, assume that v is accessible from w, and consider the atomic proposition $\{v\}$. From the perspective of w, $\{v\}$ is possible, and for every proposition p, $\{v\}$ either strictly implies p or strictly implies the negation (complement) of p. $\{v\}$ therefore satisfies a condition which we can formulate in the object language as follows, for any proposition expressed by a formula φ:

$Q(\varphi) := \Diamond\varphi \wedge \forall r(\square(\varphi \rightarrow r) \vee \square(\varphi \rightarrow \neg r))$

Here, r is some propositional variable not free in φ. If a proposition q is possible from the perspective of a world w, then it is true in some accessible world v, which means that $\{v\}$ is a proposition satisfying Q which strictly implies q. So, relational frames validate the following principle, which states that there is always such a proposition p:

(At′) $\Diamond q \rightarrow \exists p(Q(p) \wedge \square(p \rightarrow q))$

At and At′ intuitively capture aspects of the availability of atomic propositions in domains of propositional quantifiers interpreted over relational frames. We therefore call them *principles of atomicity* (an informal term which is not meant to have any precise definition). In the next section, we will see that in an NPQML with sufficiently strong modal principles, At′ follows from At in the sense that the logic contains the latter only if it contains the former. But the question how the two principles relate is much less straightforward in weaker NPQMLs. Although principles like At and At′ were already considered by Prior (1967, pp. 79–82), there does not appear to exist any systematic investigation into their relations in arbitrary NPQMLs. I therefore consider this an open problem in propositionally quantified modal logic:

Open Question 1 *In the context of which* NPQMLs *does* At *entail* At' *(and vice versa), in the sense that the logic contains the former only if it contains the latter?*

Similar questions arise for further natural principles of atomicity. These principles include a number of variants of At and At' in which □ is strengthened to a more demanding condition. By way of illustration, consider At. First, in a bimodal setting with modalities $\Box_1$ and $\Box_2$, we may not only consider an instance of At for each modality, but also the following combined principle:

$$\exists p(p \wedge \forall q(q \rightarrow \Box_1(p \rightarrow q) \wedge \Box_2(p \rightarrow q)))$$

It is easy to see that this is derivable in any NPQML containing the relevant two instances of At: if p_1 and p_2 are witnesses of At for $\Box_1$ and $\Box_2$, respectively, then $p_1 \wedge p_2$ is a witness of the combined principle. While this variant is easily seen to be derivable, the matter is different with a second variant, which iterates the modality as follows:

$$\exists p(p \wedge \forall q(q \rightarrow \Box\Box(p \rightarrow q)))$$

It is far from clear that an NPQML which contains At must also contain this iterated principle (unless, of course, it contains an iteration principle like 4).

2.5 S5 and the Reduction of Possible Worlds

In this section, we consider the special case arising from the well-known normal unimodal logic S5. S5 is strong and simple, and is often considered a contender for the correct modal logic of necessity in metaphysics. Apart from the principle T, according to which what is necessary is true, it includes the principles 4 and 5, with which it follows that being necessary and being possible are both noncontingent matters. The name "S5" is taken from Lewis and Langford (1959 [1932]), and indicates that it is the fifth in a series of systems they define, using axioms first considered by Becker (1930).

S5 can be axiomatized as KT5, or alternatively as KT4B. It defines the class E of relational frames in which the accessibility relation is an equivalence relation: a reflexive, symmetric, and transitive relation on the set of worlds. S5 is Kripke-complete, and so complete with respect to E. It is also complete with respect to the more restrictive class U of relational frames in which the accessibility relation is universal. This fits a metaphysical conception of the intended notion of necessity as being maximally broad; see Kripke (1980 [1972], p. 99) and Williamson (2013).

Unusually, the results on S5 can be extended to propositional quantifiers. First, the propositionally quantified modal logics of E and U are also the same, as we will show in Section 2.8 using the standard technique of *generated subframes*. Second, the resulting propositionally quantified modal logic also has very natural axiomatizations. Since S5 contains B, any NPQML which includes S5 already contains Bc. In Section 3.2, we will show that such an NPQML need not include the atomicity principles discussed in the last section. But the axiomatization of S5π+, that is, $\mathcal{L}^\square(R(S5))$, can be completed by adding At:

Theorem 2.5.1 S$_\Pi$5At *is sound and complete with respect to* U, *the class of relational frames with a universal accessibility relation.*

This result was shown by Kaplan (1970b) and Fine (1970). Soundness is straightforward to establish using Proposition 2.3.4. Fine notes two ways of establishing completeness: one is by a canonical model construction, and the other by a quantifier-elimination argument using certain additional logical constants. Kaplan employs the second method. Kaplan and Fine don't provide many details of these proofs, although related discussion can be found in Kaplan (1970a) and Fine (1969, 1972).

As indicated in Section 1.6, an important motivation for the investigation of S5π+ can be found in the works of Prior (1967, 1968). One of Prior's concerns was the task of giving an account of possible worlds in philosophical theorizing. Naturally, structures such as relational frames containing elements which are informally called "possible worlds" may be used for mathematical purposes without any illuminating philosophical account of possible worlds: in these contexts, possible worlds may be pure sets, or any other elements. But in many philosophical contexts, a more substantial use is made of possible worlds.

Prior considered the idea that a possible world may be considered as a proposition, namely the proposition which describes the relevant world in its entirety. According to Copeland (2006), this idea had been discussed by Prior and Meredith as early as 1953, with reference to the *Tractatus* of Wittgenstein (1921), and was stated in print in Prior (1962). The idea continued to occupy Prior's attention, and is discussed at length in work which was unfinished at the time of his death, and which was published posthumously in Prior and Fine (1977).

Using propositional quantifiers and the technical developments discussed in this section and the previous one, it is easy to see how the reduction of worlds to propositions may be carried out: Assume that S$_\Pi$5At is correct for the intended notion of necessity in the sense that all of its theorems are true under any interpretation of the free propositional variables. (As discussed by Williamson (2013, section 3.3), this is the notion of logical truth of Tarski (2002 [1936]).) Prior's idea can then be understood as proposing that talk of possible worlds can be understood as talk of propositions corresponding to possible worlds. To correspond to a possible world, a proposition has to describe a possible and complete way for things to be, that is, to be possible and to settle the truth of every proposition. In this modal context, a proposition p can be understood to settle a proposition q as being true if it strictly implies it, namely, if $\Box(p \rightarrow q)$, and to settle q as being false of it strictly implies its negation, that is, if $\Box(p \rightarrow \neg q)$. That is, a proposition p corresponds to a possible world just in case it satisfies condition Q defined in the previous section. If p is a such world-proposition, we understand a proposition q to be true in p just in case p settles q as being true, that is, just in case $\Box(p \rightarrow q)$.

We can now use $S_\Pi 5At$ to show that this way of regimenting talk of possible worlds vindicates central assumptions about the relationship between possible worlds and propositions. Most importantly, we can prove what Menzel and Zalta (2014) call the *fundamental principle of world theory*: the claim that a proposition is possible just in case it is true in some possible world. On Prior's proposal, this can be regimented as the following sentence of $\mathcal{L}^\Box$:

$$\forall q(\Diamond q \leftrightarrow \exists p(Q(p) \land \Box(p \rightarrow q)))$$

This sentence is provable in $S_\Pi 5At$: it is easy to see that it is valid on U, so the claim follows from Theorem 2.5.1.

This sketch of Prior's proposal is somewhat of a simplification: In actual fact, Prior held that the existence of propositions is in general a contingent matter. This conflicts with $S_\Pi 5At$, and in particular with certain instances of the Barcan formula and its converse. Weakening the logic to admit the contingent existence of propositions introduces substantial complications, as discussed by Fine in the postscript of Prior and Fine (1977). We return to some of these issues in Section 3.6.

Setting aside difficulties arising from contingent existence, Prior's proposal is similar to many other theories of possible worlds, which conceive of possible worlds as special propositions, states of affairs, properties, sets, classes, or various similar entities; see, for example, Plantinga (1974), Stalnaker (1976), and Adams (1981). Prior's proposal has the advantage of receiving an elegant formalization using propositional quantifiers. But as Menzel and Zalta (2014, p. 336) note, these proposals typically depend on a substantial assumption, namely that *there are* the required propositions (states of affairs/properties/...)

to play the role of worlds. This applies to Prior's proposal as well: the claim that a proposition is possible just in case it is true in some world(-proposition) depends essentially on the inclusion of the atomicity principle At. Using the models of Section 3.2, we can show that this equivalence cannot be derived in $S_\Pi 5$. This poses the question: Why think that At is (necessarily) true?

It turns out that the matter can easily be settled if a way of quantifying *plurally* over propositions is added to $\mathcal{L}_\square$. The relevant plural propositional quantifiers are analogous to the plural (first-order) quantifiers of Boolos (1984). By a variant of arguments of Gallin (1975), Fine (1980), and Menzel and Zalta (2014), it can be shown that At becomes derivable in the presence of such plural propositional quantifiers. I discuss this derivation in more detail in Fritz (2023c). This result illustrates that just as in the case of standard propositional modal languages, the restrictiveness of propositionally quantified modal languages is both a boon and a burden: it makes results like Theorem 2.5.1 possible, but also bars certain interesting arguments from being formulated. Another instance of this important lesson will be mentioned in Section 4.

Finally, it is worth noting that a reduction of possible worlds to propositions can also be carried out in the context of modal logics weaker than S5. However, further complexities arise in these settings, in particular since we may no longer be able to rely on a completeness result corresponding to Theorem 2.5.1, as we will see in the next section. For recent discussion of such more general reductions of possible worlds to propositions in higher-order languages, see Dorr et al. (2021, section 1.6) and Bacon (2024, section 7.5).

2.6 Axiomatizability

Earlier, we noted that every NPQML is axiomatizable in the sense of being the NPQML axiomatized by itself. This sense of axiomatizability is therefore uninteresting. A more interesting notion of axiomatizability is that of being *recursively enumerable*, which requires being relatively well-behaved from a computational perspective: a set of formulas Λ is recursively enumerable if there is a computer program which produces only theorems of Λ, and, for every theorem Λ, produces it after some finite number of computational steps. For example, if Γ is a finite set of axioms, then $K_\Pi \Gamma$ is recursively enumerable. So, since $S5\pi+$ can be axiomatized as $S_\Pi 5At$ (i.e., $K_\Pi T5At$), it is recursively enumerable. In fact, $S5\pi+$ is computationally even better behaved, as it is *decidable*, which means that there is a computer program which takes any formula $\varphi \in \mathcal{L}^\square$ as input, and outputs after a finite number of computational steps the answer to the question whether $\varphi \in S5\pi+$:

Theorem 2.6.1 S5π+ *is decidable.*

This result was also established by Kaplan (1970b) and Fine (1970). Fine notes that it follows from the quantifier-elimination argument used to prove completeness. As shown by Ding (2021a), this argument can be extended to show that KD45π+ is decidable as well. Fine observes that there is a second way of proving Theorem 2.6.1, which is also used by Kaplan. It proceeds by extending the *standard translation* of propositional modal logic to propositional quantifiers. The standard translation shows that propositional modal languages can be thought of as fragments of first-order languages: worlds become individuals, propositional variables become predicates, and modal operators become first-order quantifiers restricted to accessible worlds. This extends straightforwardly to propositional quantifiers, which become monadic second-order quantifiers. The translation can therefore be defined as follows, given a first-order variable x which serves as the world of evaluation of the relevant formula, and assuming that X_p is a distinct monadic second-order variable, for every propositional variable p:

$$p^x := X_p x$$
$$\bot^x := \bot$$
$$(\varphi \to \psi)^x := \varphi^x \to \psi^x$$
$$(\Box\varphi)^x := \forall y(R_\Box xy \to \varphi^y)$$
$$(\forall p\varphi)^x := \forall X_p(\varphi^x)$$

The target language of monadic second-order logic is straightforwardly interpreted over relational frames understood as standard models, with the set of worlds serving as the individual domain. By a standard abuse of notation, we are here using $R_\Box$ also as a predicate of the monadic second-order object language, taking it to be interpreted using the relation $R_\Box$ of the relevant frame.

An induction shows that a propositionally quantified formula φ is valid on a relational frame just in case its translate φ^x is valid on the frame as well, in the sense of being true under any assignment function. This means that for any class of relational frames C, $\mathcal{L}^O(C)$ can be seen as a fragment of monadic second-order logic interpreted over the frames in C. (Because of this, propositionally quantified modal logic, interpreted on relational frames, is also sometimes called "second-order propositional modal logic", for example, by Kaminski and Tiomkin (1996), ten Cate (2006), and Belardinelli et al. (2018).) This means that the former is no more complex than the latter. The decidability of S5π+ therefore follows from the decidability of the monadic second-order validities over U. When interpreted over U, any formula $R_\Box xy$ becomes trivially true, and so can be replaced by ⊤. The monadic second-order validities over U can therefore be thought of as monadic second-order logic without non-logical constants, which is well-known to be decidable, by observations going back to Löwenheim (1915).

The resulting argument for the decidability of S5π+ effectively proceeds by showing that a formula $\varphi \in \mathcal{L}^\square$ is a member of S5π+ if and only if it is valid on every frame in U up to a certain finite size determined by the syntactic complexity of φ. It thereby also naturally generalizes the proof of the decidability of S5 by Parry (1933). This mode of argument can be extended to several other strong NPQMLS, as shown by Fritz (forthcoming). To state the relevant result, let worlds w and v of a relational frame $\mathfrak{F}$ be *duplicates* if the function mapping w and v to each other, and every other world to itself, is an automorphism of the whole frame (an isomorphism from the frame to itself). Being a duplicate is an equivalence relation. Let the *diversity* of a class of frames C be the supremum – if it exists – of the numbers of equivalence classes of point-generated subframes of frames in C. It can then be shown that:

Proposition 2.6.2 *If* $\Gamma \subseteq \mathcal{L}^O$ *is finite and* R(Γ) *has finite diversity, then* $\mathcal{L}^O(\text{R}(\Gamma))$ *is decidable.*

Various decidability results can be derived from this. For example, with the fact that every normal extension of K5 is finitely axiomatizable, as shown by Nagle and Thomason (1985), it follows that $\Lambda\pi$+ is decidable for every unimodal NML Λ containing the axiom 5. The general formulation of this observation might give a misleading impression: despite its simplicity, axiom 5 is very strong, and in general only highly restrictive logics define classes of relational frames with finite diversity. In fact, the vast majority of NMLs of interest define classes of relational frames whose propositionally quantified modal logic is not recursively enumerable. Fine (1970) already noted this for several examples, including KT4, also known as S4. Fine's argument proceeds by a reduction of second-order arithmetic into the relevant NPQMLS. The details of these arguments were eventually published by Garson (1984).

Kremer (1993) notes that Fine's unaxiomatizability results can be strengthened, to show that second-order logic – i.e., the validities of a full second-order language over standard models – can be reduced to these NPQMLS. This means that from a computational perspective, these NPQMLS are equivalent to second-order logic; in technical parlance, they are *recursively isomorphic* to second-order logic (see Kremer (1993) for a definition of this concept). According to Kremer (1997b, p. 530), this stronger result was already proven by Fine and Kripke "shortly after the publication of" Fine (1970). Kaminski and Tiomkin

(1996) published a proof of a generalization of this result, which is further generalized in Fritz (forthcoming). The full result is complicated to state, but we note the following important consequence:

Proposition 2.6.3 *Any unimodal* NPQML *included in* $B\pi+$, $K2.1\pi+$, *or* $K4.2W\pi+$ *is recursively isomorphic to second-order logic.*

Here, B is KTB, K2.1 is KT4MG1J1, and K4.2W is KG1W, where the axioms not yet introduced are as follows:

M $\Box\Diamond p \rightarrow \Diamond\Box p$
G1 $\Diamond\Box p \rightarrow \Box\Diamond p$
J1 $\Box(\Box(p \rightarrow \Box p) \rightarrow p) \rightarrow p$
W $\Box(\Box p \rightarrow p) \rightarrow \Box p$

It is worth noting that K4.2W proves 4 and J1. J1 is also known as Grz; W is also known as GL, after Gödel and Löb, as it plays an important role in provability logic; see Boolos (1985).

There is one important group of NMLs which the results mentioned so far do not cover, namely those (apart from S5) containing the following axiom:

Lem_0 $\Box((p \wedge \Box p) \rightarrow q) \vee \Box((q \wedge \Box q) \rightarrow p)$

This axiom enforces a weak form of linearity on relational frames. Fine (1970) noted that the propositionally quantified unimodal logic of the singleton class containing the relational frame consisting of the natural numbers under their natural order (weak or strict) is decidable. This follows by the standard translation using the corresponding result about monadic second-order logic, which had been shown by Büchi (1962). In Fritz (forthcoming), this observation is extended to show the following result:

Proposition 2.6.4 *If* Λ *is S4.3.1 or one of its normal unimodal extensions, or* $K4.3Z$, *then* $\Lambda\pi+$ *is decidable.*

Here, S4.3.1 is $KT4\text{Lem}_0N1$ and K4.3Z is $K4\text{Lem}_0Z$, where the axioms not yet introduced are as follows:

N1 $\Box(\Box(p \rightarrow \Box p) \rightarrow p) \rightarrow (\Diamond\Box p \rightarrow p)$
Z $\Box(\Box p \rightarrow p) \rightarrow (\Diamond\Box p \rightarrow \Box p)$

N1 is also known as Dum.

Büchi's result was strengthened by Rabin (1969), and Fine (1970) asserts that this can be used to establish the decidability of S4.3π+ (with S4.3 being KT4Lem$_0$). But according to Kaminski and Tiomkin (1996), this is incorrect, as it follows from results of Shelah (1975) and Gurevich and Shelah (1983) that S4.3π+ is in fact not recursively enumerable. In Fritz (forthcoming), this observation is extended to show the following result, where K3 is KT4Lem$_0$M:

Proposition 2.6.5 *For any normal unimodal logic* Λ *included in K3,* $\Lambda\pi$+ *is not recursively enumerable.*

As the results presented here illustrate, failure of recursive enumerability is usually preserved under enlargements of the relevant class of frames, while recursive enumerability is often preserved under restrictions of the relevant class of frames. Among many NMLs Λ, the question whether $\Lambda\pi$+ is recursively enumerable therefore divides the space of NMLs into two halves, separated by what Ding (2021a) calls the *axiomatizability boundary*, where Λ is sufficiently strong to be above the boundary just in case $\Lambda\pi$+ is recursively enumerable. As noted in Fritz (forthcoming), such a boundary cannot be drawn among arbitrary NMLs, since there are cases in which Λ' extends Λ, even though $\Lambda\pi$+ is recursively enumerable while $\Lambda'\pi$+ is not. The cases of logics used to show this involve infinitely many axioms, which suggests the following apparently open question, further discussed in Fritz (forthcoming):

Open Question 2 *Are there finite sets* $\Gamma \subseteq \Delta \subseteq \mathcal{L}_{qf}^{\square}$ *such that* K$\Gamma\pi$+ *is recursively axiomatizable while* K$\Delta\pi$+ *is not?*

So far, we have only discussed unimodal logics. In the multimodal case, computational tractability becomes an even rarer phenomenon. For example, even though the unimodal logic S5 defines a class of relational frames whose propositionally quantified modal logic is decidable, once we admit two modalities $\square$ and $\boxtimes$ each governed by S5, the resulting propositionally quantified modal logic is again recursively isomorphic to second-order logic. This normal bimodal logic is known as the *fusion* of S5 with S5, and written S5 ⊗ S5. To define it, we write T$_{\boxtimes}$ for the variant of the axiom T in which $\square$ is replaced by $\boxtimes$, that is, $\boxtimes p \rightarrow p$, and similarly for other axioms and modalities. Then S5 ⊗ S5 can be defined as the normal bimodal logic KT$_{\square}$5$_{\square}$T$_{\boxtimes}$5$_{\boxtimes}$.

Proposition 2.6.6 (S5⊗S5)π+ *is recursively isomorphic to second-order logic.*

This was shown by Antonelli and Thomason (2002); proofs can also be found in Kuhn (2004) and Belardinelli et al. (2018). The result is strengthened in Fritz

(2020) to the logic of so-called *products* of two frames with a universal accessibility relation. In contrast, it is shown in Fritz (forthcoming) that if S5 ⊗ S5 is strengthened by the addition of the principle □p → ⊠p, the result of which is there called a *linear fusion*, the resulting NML defines a class of frames whose propositionally quantified modal logic is again decidable. In the case of epistemic logic, axiomatizability results have also been obtained for propositionally quantified multimodal logics involving operators of public announcement or common knowledge; see Belardinelli et al. (2016) and Belardinelli et al. (2018), respectively.

Many problems concerning the axiomatizability of propositionally quantified modal logics of classes of relational frames remain open. A number of them are noted in Fritz (forthcoming, section 7), including the following (which is only very partially addressed by the results just mentioned):

Open Question 3 *Among* NMLS Λ *such that* Λπ+ *is decidable, which fusions define classes of frames whose propositionally quantified modal logic is decidable?*

A number of variations on this question can be formulated as well, where decidability is replaced by recursive enumerability, or fusions are replaced by products.

Reflecting the literature it summarizes, this section has focused mainly on relatively coarse classifications of propositionally quantified modal logics in terms of decidability, recursive axiomatizability, and recursive isomorphism to second-order logic. It would be interesting to obtain a more fine-grained classification:

Open Question 4 *What are the computational complexity classes of the various decidable* NPQMLS?

2.7 Completeness Results

In the previous section, we saw that the propositionally quantified modal logics of many natural classes of relational frames are not recursively enumerable. So, for many propositional modal logics, the addition of propositional quantifiers introduces *essential incompleteness* with respect to the model theory of relational frames. Completeness results with respect to classes of relational frames are therefore much rarer in the presence of propositional quantifiers than in their absence.

We have already discussed the most important such completeness result, which is the completeness of S$_\Pi$5At with respect to relational frames with a universal accessibility relation. This shows that $S_\Pi 5At$ is $S5\pi+$; see Theorem 2.5.1. Recall that one proof of this result proceeds by a quantifier-elimination argument. This technique can be developed further to apply to extensions of $S5\pi+$, to prove the following result. It follows from a more general result of Ding (2018), using algebraic models which we consider in Section 3.2.

Proposition 2.7.1 *Every* NPQML *which includes* $S5\pi+$ *is complete with respect to the class of relational frames it defines.*

It is worth noting that some of these normal extensions of $S5\pi+$ are not of the form $\Lambda\pi+$, for any normal modal logic Λ. For example, we can consistently extend $S5\pi+$ using the claim that there is a contingent truth: $\exists p(p \land \neg\Box p)$. This claim is not provable in $\Lambda\pi+$, for any consistent NML Λ: by Makinson (1971), every consistent NML is valid on a one-element relational frame, in which every truth is necessary. The characterization of the extensions of S5 by Scroggs (1951) and Gärdenfors (1973) therefore requires further elaboration to be adapted to the propositionally quantified case. For such an elaboration, see Ding (2018).

Using algebraic methods, Ding (2021a) has also extended the completeness result via quantifier elimination in the other direction, of weaker NMLs, and shown the following result:

Proposition 2.7.2 $K_\Pi D45BcAt$ *is complete with respect to the class of relational frames it defines, namely, the class of relational frames with a serial, transitive and Euclidean accessibility relation.*

It is important to be clear that this result does not follow straightforwardly from anything we have observed so far: It follows from Proposition 2.6.2 that $KD45\pi+$ is decidable and so that there is some recursive way of axiomatizing it. But this does not obviously mean that $K_\Pi D45BcAt$ is such an axiomatization. In general, there is no reason to expect that for every NML $K\Gamma$, if $K\Gamma\pi+$ is decidable then it is completely axiomatized by $K_\Pi \Gamma BcAt$. Indeed, a counterexample can be found in which Γ is finite, as we now show using the case of $KT4Lem_0 J1$, which is also known as K3.1. The proof is based on an incompleteness result for first-order modal logic based on S4M, which is the result of adding M to S4, namely, KT4M. This result was already announced in Kripke (1967); a proof can be found in Hughes and Cresswell (1996, pp. 265–270).

Proposition 2.7.3 K3.1π+ *is decidable, but not completely axiomatized by* K$_\Pi$3.1BcAt *(i.e.,* K$_\Pi$T4Lem$_0$J1BcAt*).*

Proof We note that $\Diamond\forall p(p \rightarrow \Box p)$ is valid on R(S4M): Call a world of a relational frame with a reflexive accessibility relation *final* if it can only access itself. Consider any relational frame on which S4M is valid. By standard arguments, it can be shown that the accessibility relation of such a frame is reflexive, transitive, and relates every world to some final world; for details, see Chagrov and Zakharyaschev (1997, p. 82). From the last condition, the validity of $\Diamond\forall p(p \rightarrow \Box p)$ is immediate.

K3.1 is an extension of S4M, so it follows that K3.1π+ contains $\Diamond\forall p(p \rightarrow \Box p)$ as well. In Section 3.5, we will be able to show that we cannot derive this formula in K$_\Pi$3.1BcAt; see Proposition 3.5.8. So K$_\Pi$3.1BcAt is incomplete with respect to R(K3.1) (the class of relational frames it defines). And since K3.1 is a normal extension of S4.3.1, it follows by Proposition 2.6.4 that K3.1π+ is decidable. $\Box$

In light of this result, it is interesting to ask how one might provide perspicuous axiomatizations of recursively enumerable logics of the form $\Lambda\pi$+ for NMLS Λ. As noted by Ding (2021a, p. 1196) the syntactic reductions involved in quantifier-elimination arguments require very strong modal logics, and it is not to be expected that this technique is applicable to all decidable logics. Fortunately, another approach is available, which is the construction of canonical models, used by Fine (1970) to establish the completeness of S$_\Pi$5At with respect to U. In unpublished work, Yipu Li and Yifeng Ding (pc) use this technique to provide a complete axiomatization of the propositionally quantified modal logic of any class of relational frames which has finite diversity and which is defined by a set of Sahlqvist formulas Γ, in terms of Γ, Bc, At, and one further axiom.

There is an important observation to be drawn from the discussion in this section and the previous one: for many NMLS Λ, it is highly ambiguous to speak of "propositionally quantified Λ". Taking the case of S4, namely, KT4, as an example, we must distinguish between the weaker S$_\Pi$4 and the stronger S4π+. Since the former is recursively enumerable and the latter is not, there are infinitely many NPQMLS linearly ordered in strength between these two logics. All of these logics will be conservative extensions of S4, and could in this sense be counted as "propositionally quantified S4". In fact, there is even a decidable NPQML *extending* S4π+ which is a conservative extension of S4. This follows via the standard translation from the completeness of S4 with respect to a single countable reflexive and transitive tree – see Blackburn et al. (2001, pp. 353–355) – and a decidability result for monadic second-order logic on such a tree, often called SωS, by Rabin (1969). As discussed by Zach (2004), analogous observations can be made for a number of further classes of trees. Zach notes that it would be interesting to provide perspicuous axiomatizations of such logics. In similar cases, of multimodal temporal logics interpreted over the natural numbers, axiomatizations of the resulting decidable propositionally quantified modal logics are provided by Kesten and Pnueli (2002) and French and Reynolds (2003).

2.8 Model Theory

An important class of techniques in the study of modal logic concern transformations of relational frames which preserve the validity of formulas. Some of these techniques continue to be applicable in the presence of propositional quantifiers, while others become inapplicable. In this section, we consider some of the most important examples.

We start with the technique of constructing generated subframes. As Blackburn et al. (2001, p. ix) stress, one of the distinguishing features of modal logic interpreted on relational frames is *locality*: the truth of a formula in a world w only depends on the features of w and the worlds which can be reached from w by finite paths along the accessibility relations. This means that a formula is valid on a world in a frame just in case it is valid on that world in the subframe which only contains these reachable worlds. This preservation result is unaffected by the inclusion of propositional quantifiers, as noted by van Benthem (1983, p. 187). The next definition and result make this observation precise.

Definition 2.8.1 *For any relational frame* $\mathfrak{F} = \langle W, R_\square \rangle_{\square \in O}$ *and world* $w \in W$, *the* point-generated subframe $\mathfrak{F}_w$ *is* $\langle W', R'_\square \rangle_{\square \in O}$, *where*

W' *is the set of* $v \in W$ *such that there is a finite sequence* $w = w_0, w_1, \ldots, w_n = v$, *where for all* $i < n$, $w_i R_\square w_{i+1}$ *for some* $\square \in O$, *and*
$R'_\square$ *is* $R_\square \cap W' \times W'$, *for all* $\square \in O$.

Proposition 2.8.2 *For every relational frame* $\mathfrak{F}$, *world* w, *assignment function* a, *and* $\varphi \in \mathcal{L}^O$,

$$\mathfrak{F}, w, a \Vdash \varphi \text{ iff } \mathfrak{F}_w, w, a' \Vdash \varphi,$$

where a' *maps any* $p \in \Phi$ *to* $a(p) \cap W'$.

Proof By induction on the complexity of φ. $\qquad\square$

This result can be refined, by considering formulas of a certain *modal depth n* (the maximal number of nested modal operators), and subframes which include only the worlds reachable in *n* steps from the generating worlds. We won't need such a refined version here; details can be found in ten Cate (2006) and Fritz (forthcoming). With generated subframes, it is easy to see that E, the class of unimodal frames in which the accessibility relation is an equivalence relation, and 𝖀, the class of unimodal frames in which the accessibility relation is universal, have the same propositionally quantified modal logic, that is, S5π+:

Proposition 2.8.3 $\mathcal{L}^{\square}(\mathsf{E}) = \mathcal{L}^{\square}(\mathsf{U})$.

Proof ⊆ is immediate, so assume that $\varphi \notin \mathcal{L}^{\square}(\mathsf{E})$. Then there is a frame $\mathfrak{F}$ in E such that $\mathfrak{F} \nVDash \varphi$. Let w be a world witnessing $\mathfrak{F} \nVDash \varphi$; by Proposition 2.8.2, $\mathfrak{F}_w \nVDash \varphi$. The worlds of $\mathfrak{F}_w$ are the members of the equivalence class of w, so $\mathfrak{F}_w$ is in U. Thus $\varphi \notin \mathcal{L}^{\square}(\mathsf{U})$.   □

As a contrast, we now consider *bounded morphisms*, also known as *pseudo-epimorphism* or *p-morphism*. A bounded morphism is a certain kind of function from one frame to another; if it is surjective (onto), it can be shown that any propositional modal formula valid on the former frame is valid on the latter frame. It turns out that this result breaks down when propositional quantifiers are included. Thus, bounded morphisms do not play an important role in propositionally quantified modal logic. We therefore skip a general definition of this concept, and only consider a pair of frames which are easily shown to be related by a bounded morphism: Let $\mathfrak{F}$ and $\mathfrak{F}'$ be unimodal relational frames whose accessibility relations are universal, with $\mathfrak{F}$ containing two worlds and $\mathfrak{F}'$ containing one world. There is just one function mapping the worlds of $\mathfrak{F}$ to the world of $\mathfrak{F}'$, and it is a surjective bounded morphism. Consequently, every propositional modal formula valid on $\mathfrak{F}$ is valid on $\mathfrak{F}'$. It is easy to see that this does not hold for formulas with propositional quantifiers: $\exists p(p \wedge \neg \square p)$ is valid on $\mathfrak{F}$ but not valid on $\mathfrak{F}'$.

The case of bounded morphisms illustrates that propositional modal languages become more expressive when propositional quantifiers are added. This idea can be made more precise by considering the notion of a modally definable class of frames: a class of relational frames C is *definable* in a given language $\mathcal{L}$ if there is a set of formulas Γ of $\mathcal{L}$ which defines C. A well-known case of a class of relational frames which is not definable in $\mathcal{L}^{\square}_{\mathrm{qf}}$ is the class of frames in which the accessibility relation is irreflexive. This is easy to define with propositional quantifiers, using the formula $\exists p(\square p \wedge \neg p)$. Yet, even with propositional quantifiers, not every class of frames is definable. This follows already by cardinality considerations, but we can also note a concrete example: by Proposition 2.8.3, U is not definable in $\mathcal{L}^\square$, but it is easily defined in first-order logic (considering relational frames as models of first-order logic as in the discussion of the standard translation in Section 2.6). A more detailed investigation of the classes of relational frames definable in $\mathcal{L}^\square$, along with a prenex normal form theorem, can be found in ten Cate (2006). For a closer look at propositionally quantified formulas expressing first-order conditions on relational frames, see Zhao (2023).

Bounded morphisms are closely related to bisimulations. A bisimulation is a certain kind of relation between the worlds of two relational models (i.e., frames with assignment functions) which guarantees that the same formulas of $\mathcal{L}_{qf}$ are true in any two connected worlds. As in the case of bounded morphisms, this guarantee does not extend to formulas of $\mathcal{L}$ involving quantifiers. However, the definition of a bisimulation can be adapted in a natural way to take into account the additional resources of propositional quantifiers. Such a variant definition can be found in Fritz (forthcoming, section 3.3); a related notion is presented in Belardinelli et al. (2018, section 5.1). It is also possible to provide a different way of interpreting $\forall p$ and $\exists p$ on relational frames which makes them invariant under bisimulation; see French (2006) and Steinsvold (2020). The resulting notion of *bisimulation quantifiers* is connected to the study of the modal μ-calculus, which also extends propositional modal logics by quantifier-like connectives. These connectives are written as μp and νp, and interpreted in terms of fixed points; for more, see Bradfield and Stirling (2007).

3 Beyond Relational Frames

3.1 Neighborhood Frames

We begin our exploration of further models for propositionally quantified modal logics with a number of generalizations of relational frames. These generalizations are well known in the quantifier-free case; see Segerberg (1971) and Hansson and Gärdenfors (1973) for illuminating general discussion. In many cases, these models have not been considered in the presence of propositional quantifiers, and many fundamental questions remain open. We start with neighborhood frames. Neighborhood frames are also known as *Scott-Montague frames*, after Scott (1970) and Montague (1970). Chellas (1980) calls them *minimal models*. A detailed discussion of them can be found in Pacuit (2017).

Neighborhood frames arise as a natural generalization of relational frames. First, note that relational frames specify, for each world w, which propositions fall under any given modality $\square$, namely those propositions (i.e., sets of worlds) which include $R_\square(w)$, the set of worlds accessible via the relation for $\square$.

This puts various constraints on the set of propositions which fall under the modality □ at any given world. For example, for every world w, the set of propositions which include $R_\square(w)$ is closed under conjunction (i.e., intersection). The resulting constraints ensure that the logic of any class of relational frames is normal.

However, in various applications, normality is undesired. For example, you might endorse an epistemic theory on which knowledge is not closed under conjunction, so that an agent might know p and know q, without knowing $p \wedge q$. This is an instance of a much-debated principle of closure in epistemology; see Hawthorne (2004) for in-depth discussion. Similarly, a deontic theory might deny that an obligation to bring p about entails an obligation to bring $p \vee q$ about, which is another entailment licensed by normal modal logics. A well-known example for this is due to Ross (1941), who notes that it does not seem to follow from an agent being obliged to post a letter that the agent is obliged to post it or burn it.

To obtain models which don't underwrite these inferences of normal modal logics, we should allow for the set of propositions which are determined to fall under □ not to obey the relevant closure conditions. The simplest way to introduce this flexibility is to specify directly as part of the model which propositions fall under □ at a given world. So, instead of an accessibility relation $R_\square$, we may simply use a function $N_\square$ which maps every world w to the set of propositions which fall under □ at w. For historical reasons to do with connections to topology, to which we return shortly, such a function $N_\square$ is known as a neighborhood function, from which the terminology of neighborhood frames is derived.

Relational frames can straightforwardly be understood as a special case of neighborhood frames, since every accessibility relation $R_\square$ corresponds to a unique neighborhood function, namely the function which maps every world w to the set of propositions which include $R_\square(w)$. When convenient, we will therefore treat relational frames as (special) neighborhood frames. It is also easy to see that not every neighborhood function $N_\square$ can be obtained from an accessibility relation $R_\square$ in the way just indicated: for example, let $N_\square(w)$ be empty for every world w of a non-empty set W. Further, the resulting neighborhood frame will fail to validate □⊤, and so its logic will not be normal.

Neighborhood frames generalize straightforwardly to polyadic modal operators: If ∘ is an n-ary modal operator, then the neighborhood function for ∘ maps each world w to a set of sequences of propositions of length n, containing those sequences of propositions which are to be related by ∘ at w. Similar to relational frames in the unary case, many possible worlds model theories of polyadic modal operators can be understood as special cases of neighborhood frames. Examples include the many model theories of counterfactuals based on possible worlds, such as those of Stalnaker (1968) and Lewis (1973). For discussions of propositional quantifiers in such a context, see Lewis (1973, pp. 45–47) and Besnard et al. (1997).

Having motivated neighborhood frames conceptually, we define them as follows:

Definition 3.1.1 *A neighborhood frame (for a modal signature $\sigma = \langle O, \rho \rangle$) is a structure $\mathfrak{F} = \langle W, N_\circ \rangle_{\circ \in O}$ such that W is a set and $N_\circ : W \to \mathcal{P}(\mathcal{P}(W)^{\rho(\circ)})$ for every $\circ \in O$. Assignment functions, truth, and validity are all defined as in Definition 2.3.1, with the exception of the recursive clause for truth of modal formulas, which is now as follows:*

$$\mathfrak{F}, w, a \Vdash \circ \varphi_1 \ldots \varphi_n \text{ if and only if } \langle [\![\varphi_1]\!]_{\mathfrak{F},a}, \ldots, [\![\varphi_n]\!]_{\mathfrak{F},a} \rangle \in N_\circ(w),$$

where $n = \rho(\circ)$ and $[\![\varphi_i]\!]_{\mathfrak{F},a} = \{v \in W : \mathfrak{F}, v, a \Vdash \varphi_i\}$.

We write N for the class of all neighborhood frames (for a given modal signature).

Although neighborhood frames do not enforce the principles of normality, they do impose constraints which go beyond those captured by classicality as defined in Section 2.2. It turns out that the principal constraint imposed on the logic of any class of neighborhood frames is that if it is valid on the class that two formulas are materially equivalent, then these formulas can be replaced in any context without changing the validity of the surrounding formula. Adapting terminology from algebra, we call this feature *congruentiality*. (Recall from Section 2.2 that "classical" is sometimes used instead of "congruential", a usage which we don't follow since we require the label "classical" for a weaker condition.) Formally, this constraint can be formulated as follows:

Definition 3.1.2 *For any set $\Lambda \subseteq \mathcal{L}^\sigma$, we define the following condition:*

(Cong) *If $\circ \in O$, $n = \rho(\circ)$, and $\varphi_i \leftrightarrow \psi_i \in \Lambda$ for all $i < n$, then*

$$\circ \varphi_0 \ldots \varphi_{n-1} \leftrightarrow \circ \psi_0 \ldots \psi_{n-1} \in \Lambda.$$

Λ *is a* congruential (propositionally quantified) modal logic *if it is a classical (propositionally quantified) modal logic satisfying* Cong.

Analogous to the normal case, we abbreviate "congruential (propositionally quantified) modal logic" as "CML" ("CPQML"). Further, the standard result that the modal logic of any class of neighborhood frames is congruential can be extended to the propositionally quantified case, as the following proposition notes:

Proposition 3.1.3 *For any class* C *of neighborhood frames,* $\mathcal{L}^\sigma(\mathsf{C})$ *is a* CPQML.

Proof Analogous to the proof of Proposition 2.3.4, considering Cong instead of K and Nec. □

Finally, we introduce – as in the normal case – labels for congruential logics axiomatized by any given set of formulas:

Definition 3.1.4 *For any set* $\Gamma \subseteq \mathcal{L}^\sigma_{qf}$, *the* CML *axiomatized by* Γ, *written* $\mathsf{E}^\sigma \Gamma$, *is the smallest* CML *including* Γ. *For any set* $\Gamma \subseteq \mathcal{L}^\sigma$, *the* CPQML *axiomatized by* Γ, *written* $\mathsf{E}^\sigma_\Pi \Gamma$, *is the smallest* CPQML *including* Γ.

Neighborhood frames relate to CMLs in very much the same way in which relational frames relate to NMLs. We have already seen Proposition 3.1.3, which corresponds to Proposition 2.3.4. E is also complete with respect to N, just as K is complete with respect to R. Furthermore, Gerson (1975b) showed that there are CMLs which are not sound and complete with respect to any class of neighborhood frames, just as there are NMLs which are not sound and complete with respect to any class of relational frames.

Turning to propositionally quantified modal logics, the corresponding completeness question with respect to arbitrary neighborhood frames appears not to have been considered. Some basic observations are easily made. We start with the two schematic principles discussed in Section 2.4. First, even though the domain of propositional quantification is still independent of the world of evaluation, the Barcan formula Bc can be falsified on neighborhood frames. In fact, the same applies to instances of the converse Barcan formula, which are derivable in NPQMLs. These observations mirror corresponding results concerning neighborhood semantics for modal predicate logic; see Arló Costa (2002) and Pacuit (2017, section 3.2). Second, the atomicity principle At (for any modality □) is also not valid on all neighborhood frames.

Proposition 3.1.5 *None of the following formulas is valid on* N:

(i) $\Box \forall p \Box p \to \forall p \Box \Box p$ *(an instance of the converse of* Bc)
(ii) $\forall p \Box \Box p \to \Box \forall p \Box p$ *(an instance of* Bc)
(iii) $\exists p(p \wedge \forall q(q \to \Box(p \to q)))$ *(i.e., any instance of* At)

Proof Let $W = \{0, 1\}$. For each formula, we construct a neighborhood frame on W on which it can be falsified. For (i), interpret □ as negation, that is, let $N_\Box(w) = \{x \subseteq W : w \notin x\}$ for all $w \in W$; then (i) is false in every world. For (ii), let $N_\Box(0) = \{\emptyset, W\}$ and $N_\Box(1) = \{\{0\}, \{1\}\}$; then (ii) is false in 1. For (iii), let $N_\Box(w) = \emptyset$ for all $w \in W$; then (iii) is false in every world. □

With none of the formulas of Section 2.4 being valid on all neighborhood frames, it is natural to wonder whether E_Π is complete with respect to N. But this can easily be shown not to be the case. First, $\Box\top \to$ At is valid on N for every unary modality $\Box$: if $\Box\top$ is true in a world w, then $\{w\}$ again witnesses the truth of At. Second, we will see in the next sections that there are extensions of E_Π which are normal, and therefore contain $\Box\top$, but which do not contain At. Any formula of the form $\Box\top \to$ At is therefore an example of the incompleteness of E_Π with respect to N. In fact, $\mathcal{L}^\Box(N)$ is not recursively enumerable. We return to this observation at the end of this section, when we will be able to derive it from a corresponding result, due to Kremer (1997c), for a more restricted class of frames which we will encounter shortly.

So far, we have considered two ways in which neighborhood frames offer greater flexibility than relational frames: First, they weaken the logical constraints, allowing us to extend our scope from normal to congruential modal logics. Second, they very naturally extend to polyadic modal operators. There is a third way in which neighborhood frames offer greater flexibility than relational frames: there are *normal* unimodal logics which are not sound and complete with respect to any class of relational frames, but sound and complete with respect to classes of neighborhood frames. This was shown by Gerson (1975a, 1976). Nevertheless, there are also normal unimodal logics which are not sound and complete with respect to any classes of *neighborhood* frames, which was also shown by Gerson (1975b).

Neighborhood frames whose logic is normal are easily characterized using the standard order-theoretic notion of a filter on a powerset. A set $F \subseteq \mathcal{P}(W)$ is a *filter* just in case the following three conditions are satisfied:

(i) $W \in F$
(ii) If $x \in F$ and $y \in F$, then $x \cap y \in F$.
(iii) If $x \in F$ and $y \subseteq W$, then $x \cup y \in F$.

For any unary modal signature O, let a neighborhood frame $\mathfrak{F} = \langle W, N_\Box \rangle_{\Box \in O}$ be a *filter neighborhood frame* just in case for every $\Box \in O$ and $w \in W$, $N_\Box(w)$ is a filter. Let F be the class of filter neighborhood frames.

Proposition 3.1.6 *A neighborhood frame* $\mathfrak{F} = \langle W, N_\Box \rangle_{\Box \in O}$ *for a unary modal signature O is a filter neighborhood frame if and only if the $\mathcal{L}^O_{qf}$-formulas valid on $\mathfrak{F}$ form an* NML *(in which case the $\mathcal{L}^O$-formulas valid on $\mathfrak{F}$ form an* NPQML*).*

Proof The left-to-right direction follows from the fact that if $\mathfrak{F}$ is filter neighborhood frame, then $W \in N_\Box(w)$, and $(W \setminus x) \cup y, x \in N_\Box(w)$ only if $y \in N_\Box(w)$, for all $w \in W$ and $x, y \subseteq W$. The right-to-left direction follows from the fact that every NML contains $\Box\top$, $(\Box p \wedge \Box q) \to \Box(p \wedge q)$, and $\Box p \to \Box(p \vee q)$. $\quad\square$

What kinds of NPQMLs are determined by classes of filter neighborhood frames? Since the logic of any filter neighborhood frame is normal, it follows with the derivability of the converse Barcan formula in NPQMLs that any instance of this schema is also valid on any class of filter neighborhood frames. Furthermore, it is easy to see that every instance of At is also valid on any such class: as in the case of relational frames, the relevant existential claim is always witnessed by the singleton of the world of evaluation. This tells us that despite Proposition 3.1.5 (iii), neighborhood frames cannot be used to construct a model theory for any NPQML which does not include At. The matter is different for the Barcan formula, as the following proposition shows:

Proposition 3.1.7 *The following instance of* Bc *is not valid on* F:

$$\forall p \Box (\Box p \to p) \to \Box \forall p (\Box p \to p)$$

Proof Let $\mathfrak{F}$ be the neighborhood frame $\langle \mathbb{N}, N_\Box \rangle$, where for each $n \in \mathbb{N}$, $N_\Box(n)$ is the set of cofinite subsets of $\mathbb{N}$, that is, the set of $x \subseteq \mathbb{N}$ such that $\mathbb{N} \backslash x$ is finite. Since the cofinite sets form a filter, $\mathfrak{F}$ is a filter neighborhood frame.

$[\![\Box p \to p]\!]_{\mathfrak{F},a}$ is cofinite, whether $a(p)$ is cofinite or not. So $\mathfrak{F} \Vdash \forall p \Box (\Box p \to p)$. However, if $a(p) = \mathbb{N} \backslash \{n\}$, then $\mathfrak{F}, n, a \nVdash \Box p \to p$. So, $\mathfrak{F} \Vdash \neg \forall p (\Box p \to p)$, whence $\mathfrak{F} \Vdash \neg \Box \forall p (\Box p \to p)$. Thus $\mathfrak{F} \nVdash \forall p \Box (\Box p \to p) \to \Box \forall p (\Box p \to p)$. □

As we noted earlier, relational frames can be thought of as a special class of (filter) neighborhood frames. Many other kinds of possible worlds model theories of modal languages can be thought of as special classes of neighborhood frames as well. Another example is the case of topologies, used as models of propositional languages with one unary modal operator. Such models in fact predate relational frames, going back to Tang (1938), McKinsey (1941), and McKinsey and Tarski (1944). This topological interpretation is especially interesting for us, since Kremer (1997c, 2018) has investigated them as models of $\mathcal{L}^\Box$.

For our purposes, it will suffice to introduce just the basic ideas. More on topology in general can be found in textbooks like Dugundji (1966); for an overview of topological modal logic see van Benthem and Bezhanishvili (2007); and for a discussion of topological model in the context of neighborhood frames see Pacuit (2017, section 1.4.1). Similar to the notion of a filter, a *topological space* on a set W is a set $T \subseteq \mathcal{P}(W)$ satisfying the following three conditions:

(i) $W \in T$ and $\emptyset \in T$.
(ii) If X is a finite subset of T, then $\bigcap X \in T$.
(iii) If X is a subset of T, then $\bigcup X \in T$.

Such a topological space can be understood as determining a neighborhood frame, namely the frame $\langle W, N_\square \rangle$, where for all $x \subseteq W$ and $w \in W$:

$$x \in N_\square(w) \text{ if and only if } w \in s \subseteq x \text{ for some } s \in T$$

(In topological terms, and adopting the algebraic perspective which we will consider in the next section, this means that $\square$ is interpreted as the interior operation of the topological space.) Let T be the class of neighborhood frames determined by topological spaces. All such frames are filter neighborhood frames; moreover, the modal logic of T turns out to be exactly S4.

Kremer (1997c) introduces the label S4πt for $\mathcal{L}^\square(T)$. His results entail the following proper inclusions:

Proposition 3.1.8 $S_\Pi 4At \subsetneq S4\pi t \subsetneq S4\pi+$.

The improper inclusions are easy corollaries of results which we have already noted. That S4πt is a proper subset of S4π+ follows from Kremer's observation that certain instances of Bc are not valid on T. That $S_\Pi 4At$ is a proper subset of S4πt follows from the following result, which Kremer establishes by reducing second-order arithmetic to S4πt, together with the obvious fact that $S_\Pi 4At$ is recursively enumerable:

Proposition 3.1.9 *S4πt is not recursively enumerable.*

This is the result we can use to establish that $\mathcal{L}(N)$ is not recursively axiomatizable, since $\mathcal{L}(T)$ is reducible to $\mathcal{L}(N)$, in the sense that there is a computable function $f: \mathcal{L} \to \mathcal{L}$ such that $\varphi \in \mathcal{L}(T)$ if and only if $f(\varphi) \in \mathcal{L}(N)$. In fact, $\mathcal{L}(T)$ is reducible to the logic of any class of neighborhood frames which includes all (neighborhood frames determined by) topological spaces. The class of filter neighborhood frames F is another example of such a class we have encountered.

The reduction itself is easy to define. First, we introduce a formula which encodes that the axiomatic principles of S4 hold on any interpretation of the proposition letters:

(ρ_{S4}) $\forall p \forall q (\square\top \wedge (\square(p \to q) \to (\square p \to \square q)) \wedge (\square p \to p) \wedge (\square p \to \square\square p))$

In the context of congruential modal logics, $\square\top$ corresponds to the rule of necessitation; the four conjuncts therefore correspond to the rule of necessitation and the axioms K, T and 4. Let $\cdot^*$ be the recursive mapping from $\mathcal{L}^\square$ to $\mathcal{L}^\square$ whose only nontrivial condition is:

$(\square\varphi)^* := \square(\rho_{S4} \to \varphi^*)$

Finally, let $\varphi^\dagger := \rho_{S4} \to \varphi^*$. We will show that $\cdot^\dagger$ reduces $\mathcal{L}(\mathsf{T})$ to $\mathcal{L}(\mathsf{N})$.

To do so, we require a way of restricting any neighborhood frame to worlds which validate ρ_{S4}. So, for any neighborhood frame $\mathfrak{F} = \langle W, N \rangle$, let $\mathfrak{F}^{S4}$ be the neighborhood frame $\langle W', N' \rangle$, such that:

$$W' = [\![\rho_{S4}]\!]_\mathfrak{F}$$
$$N'(w) = \{x \cap W' : x \in N(w)\}$$

The central claims needed to establish the reduction are collected in the following lemma:

Lemma 3.1.10 *Let $\mathfrak{F} = \langle W, N \rangle$ be a neighborhood frame.*

(i) $\mathfrak{F} \Vdash \rho_{S4}$ if and only if $\mathfrak{F}$ is in T.

(ii) For all $w \in W'$ and assignment functions a, $\mathfrak{F}, w, a \Vdash \varphi^*$ if and only if $\mathfrak{F}^{S4}, w, a' \Vdash \varphi$, where $a'(p) = a(p) \cap W'$, for all $p \in \Phi$.

(iii) $\mathfrak{F}^{S4} \Vdash \rho_{S4}$, whence $\mathfrak{F}^{S4}$ is in T (by i).

Proof (i) follows from Pacuit (2017, p. 24, proposition 1.1).

(ii) By induction on the complexity of φ.

(iii) Considering the four conjuncts individually, using ii. □

Although this won't be needed in the following, it is worth noting that ρ_{S4} is valid on a neighborhood frame just in case S4 is valid on it. With the three results of Lemma 3.1.10, the reduction follows:

Proposition 3.1.11 *For every class C of neighborhood frames which includes T, $\mathcal{L}(\mathsf{T})$ is reducible to $\mathcal{L}(\mathsf{C})$.*

Proof We show, for any $\varphi \in \mathcal{L}^\square$, that $\varphi \in \mathcal{L}(\mathsf{T})$ if and only if $\varphi^\dagger \in \mathcal{L}(\mathsf{C})$.

If $\varphi \notin \mathcal{L}(\mathsf{T})$, then there is a neighborhood frame $\mathfrak{F}$ in T (i.e., a topological space), on which φ is not valid. By Lemma 3.1.10(i), ρ_{S4} is valid on $\mathfrak{F}$. Consequently, $\mathfrak{F}^{S4}$ is $\mathfrak{F}$, and so by Lemma 3.1.10(ii), φ^* fails to be valid on $\mathfrak{F}$ as well. Since C includes T, $\varphi^\dagger \notin \mathcal{L}(\mathsf{C})$.

If $\varphi^\dagger \notin \mathcal{L}(\mathsf{C})$, then there is a neighborhood frame $\mathfrak{F}$, world w, and assignment function a such that $\mathfrak{F}, w, a \nVdash \varphi^\dagger$. First, it follows that $\mathfrak{F}, w, a \Vdash \rho_{S4}$, which means that w is contained in $\mathfrak{F}^{S4}$, and with Lemma 3.1.10(iii), that $\mathfrak{F}^{S4}$ is in T. Second, $\mathfrak{F}, w, a \nVdash \varphi^*$; since w is contained in $\mathfrak{F}^{S4}$, it follows with Lemma 3.1.10(ii) that $\mathfrak{F}^{S4}, w, a' \nVdash \varphi$. Thus $\varphi \notin \mathcal{L}(\mathsf{T})$. □

Using Kremer's result stated earlier as Proposition 3.1.9, we obtain:

Corollary 3.1.12 *Neither $\mathcal{L}(\mathsf{N})$ nor $\mathcal{L}(\mathsf{F})$ is recursively axiomatizable.*

As Kremer notes, it is an open question whether his result can be strengthened to recursive isomorphism to second-order logic:

Open Question 5 *Is S4πt recursively isomorphic to second-order logic?*

Given our observations here, a positive answer will settle the matter as well for $\mathcal{L}(N)$ and $\mathcal{L}(F)$. If the answer is negative, separate analogous questions arise for these logics.

3.2 Complete Boolean Algebras

Our next generalization of relational frames exchanges the representation of propositions by sets of possible worlds with a more abstract, algebraic, structure. To motivate this idea, it is helpful to consider a variant definition of neighborhood frames, which is mathematically equivalent to the one presented earlier. Recall that neighborhood frames simply stipulate, for each world and modality of arity n, which sequences of propositions (sets of worlds) of length n are related by the modality at that world. Equivalently, we can think of a neighborhood frame as stipulating, for each modality of arity n and sequence of propositions of length n, at which worlds these propositions are related by that modality. The set of these worlds can be thought of as *the proposition that these proposition are related by that modality*. So, formally, a neighborhood function $N_\circ$ for a modality $\circ$ of arity n can also be represented as a function $*_\circ$ mapping any sequence of n propositions to a proposition. It is easy to see that every neighborhood function $N_\circ$ determines a unique function $*_\circ$, and vice versa. To illustrate this informally, if $\Box$ is interpreted as *being known* (by a certain agent), then the relevant function $*_\Box$ can be understood as mapping every proposition x to the proposition that x is known.

A neighborhood frame can therefore equivalently be presented as a structure $\langle W, *_\circ \rangle_{\circ \in O}$, where W is a set and $*_\circ$ is a function from $\mathcal{P}(W)^{\rho(\circ)}$ to $\mathcal{P}(W)$, for all $\circ \in O$. On this presentation, the evaluation clause for modal operators turns into the following condition:

$$\mathfrak{F}, w, a \Vdash \circ\varphi_1 \ldots \varphi_n \text{ if and only if } w \in *_\circ(\langle [\![\varphi_1]\!]_{\mathfrak{F},a}, \ldots, [\![\varphi_n]\!]_{\mathfrak{F},a}\rangle).$$

In fact, on this presentation of neighborhood frames, it makes sense not to take the relation of truth $\Vdash$ as basic and define the interpretation function $[\![\cdot]\!]_\circ$ in terms of it, but to reverse the order: That is, it makes sense to recursively define a function $[\![\cdot]\!]_\circ$ which assigns to each formula the proposition it expresses, and then derive the truth relation $\Vdash$ by saying that $\mathfrak{F}, w, a \Vdash \varphi$ if and only if $w \in [\![\varphi]\!]_{\mathfrak{F},a}$. The clause for a modality $\circ$ then becomes a simple application of the function $*_\circ$ used to interpret it:

$$[\![\circ\varphi_1 \ldots \varphi_n]\!]_{\mathfrak{F},a} = *_\circ(\langle [\![\varphi_1]\!]_{\mathfrak{F},a}, \ldots, [\![\varphi_n]\!]_{\mathfrak{F},a} \rangle)$$

This makes clear that neighborhood semantics is in one sense a maximally permissive generalization of relational frames: modal operators are interpreted using *completely arbitrary* functions on propositions.

The other truth-conditional clauses can be given a corresponding presentation in terms of the interpretation function, with Boolean connectives interpreted using corresponding set-theoretic operations. If we used $\neg$ and $\wedge$ as the primitive Boolean connectives, these would be the operations of complement relative to the set of worlds, and intersection, respectively. The choice of $\bot$ and $\rightarrow$ as primitive makes the corresponding operations unfortunately somewhat less intuitive:

$$[\![p]\!]_{\mathfrak{F},a} = a(p)$$
$$[\![\bot]\!]_{\mathfrak{F},a} = \emptyset$$
$$[\![\varphi \rightarrow \psi]\!]_{\mathfrak{F},a} = (W \setminus [\![\varphi]\!]_{\mathfrak{F},a}) \cup [\![\psi]\!]_{\mathfrak{F},a}$$

We focus just on the quantifier-free setting for the moment, and get back to quantifiers shortly.

We have arrived at an *algebraic* perspective on neighborhood frames. (For more on algebraic approaches to logic, see Halmos and Givant (1998), Dunn and Hardegree (2001), and Rasiowa and Sikorski (1963).) Let a *powerset algebra* be a structure $\mathfrak{A} = \langle A, 0, \sqsupset \rangle$, where $A = \mathcal{P}(W)$ for some set W, $0 = \emptyset$, and $x \sqsupset y = (W \setminus x) \cup y$ for all $x, y \subseteq W$. (Here, "0" need not stand for the number zero; context will always disambiguate between the algebraic and numerical reading.) From an algebraic perspective, we can think of a neighborhood frame as extending a powerset algebra by arbitrary n-ary functions on the underlying powerset. Once the set-theoretic operations are explicitly represented in the algebra, the set-theoretic nature of the elements of the algebra becomes immaterial. Instead of neighborhood frames, we can therefore equivalently consider any algebra isomorphic to a powerset algebra, extended by arbitrary polyadic functions on the underlying set. This raises the question: which structural constraints are imposed by requiring an algebra $\langle A, 0, \sqsupset \rangle$ to be isomorphic to a powerset algebra? The well-known answer to this question is the following:

Proposition 3.2.1 *An algebra $\langle A, 0, \sqsupset \rangle$ is isomorphic to a powerset algebra if and only if it is a complete atomic Boolean algebra.*

For a proof, and rigorous definition of the relevant algebraic concepts, see a textbook treating Boolean algebras, such as Davey and Priestley (2002) and Givant and Halmos (2009). Here, we will have to limit ourselves to a brief discussion of these concepts. First, we can think of a Boolean algebra as an algebra

$\mathfrak{A} = \langle A, 0, \sqsupset \rangle$, where A is a set, $0 \in A$, and $\sqsupset$ a binary function on A, such that on the present interpretation of Boolean formulas on such an algebra, any two formulas which are equivalent by classical propositional logic are interpreted as the same element of the algebra. As a consequence, we can define, in any Boolean algebra, operations $-$, $\sqcup$, and $\sqcap$ which interpret $\neg$, $\lor$, and $\land$, as well as a distinguished element 1 interpreting $\top$. For example, $-$ is defined as mapping x to $x \sqsupset 0$, and 1 is defined as -0.

It remains to define completeness and atomicity. For completeness, we first define an order $\leq$ among elements of A, stipulating that $x \leq y$ if and only if $x = x \land y$. This order is sometimes called *entailment*, but note that it is a relation among elements of the algebra, which represent propositions, and not among formulas. Intuitively, it orders propositions according to strength, so that $x \leq y$ just in case x is at least as strong as y. It can be shown that $\leq$ is a *partial order*, which means that it is reflexive, transitive, and antisymmetric. (See Davey and Priestley (2002) for definitions of such basic order-theoretic notions.) Furthermore, it can be shown that $\leq$ forms a *lattice*, which means that any two elements x and y have a least upper bound and a greatest lower bound. $\mathfrak{A}$ is *complete* just in case every set $X \subseteq A$ has a least upper bound and a greatest lower bound. For atomicity, an element a of A is defined as an *atom* just in case a is distinct from 0, and there is no other element $x \in A$ such that $x \leq a$. $\mathfrak{A}$ is *atomic* just in case for every $x \neq 0$, there is an atom $a \leq x$.

The requirement for $\mathfrak{A}$ to be Boolean ensures that every theorem of classical propositional logic is always interpreted as the top element 1, under any interpretation of the proposition letters, which is the algebraic correspondent of the notion of being valid on a frame. Requiring $\mathfrak{A}$ to be Boolean therefore plays a crucial role in ensuring the validity of tautologies. (Although see Section 4 for less restrictive ways of achieving this end.) It turns out that the constraints of completeness and atomicity are not required to guarantee the principles of CMLs. So, using the algebraic perspective, we can generalize the class of neighborhood frames simply by dropping the requirement for the underlying Boolean algebra to be complete and atomic. More formally, we therefore make the following definition:

Definition 3.2.2 *A* Boolean algebra expansion *(for a modal signature* $\sigma = \langle O, \rho \rangle$*) is a structure* $\mathfrak{A} = \langle A, 0, \sqsupset, *_\circ \rangle_{\circ \in O}$ *such that* $\langle A, 0, \sqsupset \rangle$ *is a Boolean algebra and* $*_\circ : A^{\rho(\circ)} \to A$ *for every* $\circ \in O$. *An* assignment function *is a function* $a: \Phi \to A$. *The interpretation of quantifier-free formulas is defined recursively using the following clauses:*

$[\![p]\!]_{\mathfrak{A},a} = a(p)$

$[\![\bot]\!]_{\mathfrak{A},a} = 0$

$[\![\varphi \rightarrow \psi]\!]_{\mathfrak{A},a} = [\![\varphi]\!]_{\mathfrak{A},a} \sqsupset [\![\psi]\!]_{\mathfrak{A},a}$

$[\![\circ\varphi_1 \ldots \varphi_n]\!]_{\mathfrak{A},a} = *_\circ(\langle [\![\varphi_1]\!]_{\mathfrak{A},a}, \ldots, [\![\varphi_n]\!]_{\mathfrak{A},a}\rangle)$

Validity *is defined by letting* $\mathfrak{A} \Vdash \varphi$ *if* $[\![\varphi]\!]_{\mathfrak{A},a} = 1$ *for all* $a \colon \Phi \rightarrow A$.

The label of "Boolean algebra expansion" is taken from Ding and Holliday (2020). We abbreviate it using "BAE" in the following. As in the case of neighborhood frames, the logic of every class of BAEs is a CML. However, unlike the case of neighborhood frames, the converse holds for BAEs: every CML is the logic of some class of BAEs. This is straightforward to show, using the standard construction of a Lindenbaum–Tarski algebra. In the terminology of Chagrov and Zakharyaschev (1997), BAEs therefore provide an "adequate" model theory of CMLS.

We are finally ready to return to languages involving propositional quantifiers. First, note that the evaluation clause of propositional quantifiers in neighborhood frames can equivalently be formulated by stating that the proposition expressed by a universal propositional quantification is the conjunction (intersection) of its instances:

$$[\![\forall p\varphi]\!]_{\mathfrak{F},a} = \bigcap_{x \in \mathcal{P}(W)} [\![\varphi]\!]_{\mathfrak{F},a[x/p]}$$

In a powerset $\mathcal{P}(W)$, the intersection of any set $X \subseteq \mathcal{P}(W)$ is its greatest lower bound (under the entailment order $\leq$). This fits well with the common idea that universal quantifications are conjunctions of their instances, and the fact that the binary conjunction operation $\sqcap$ in Boolean algebras maps any two elements to their greatest lower bound. This suggests that algebraically, propositional quantifiers can be interpreted using greatest lower bounds as well. In the following, we notate greatest lower bounds using $\bigwedge$. We must, of course, ensure that the relevant greatest lower bounds always exist. The simplest way to do so is to assume that the algebra is complete, in the sense defined earlier. (We consider a weaker, but more complicated, requirement in Section 3.4.) With this, Definition 3.2.2 is straightforwardly extended to propositional quantifiers, at least for *complete* BAEs, which we call CBAEs. (We extend properties of Boolean algebras to BAEs in the obvious way; for example, a BAE is complete just in case its underlying Boolean algebra is complete.)

Definition 3.2.3 *For any* CBAE $\mathfrak{A} = \langle A, 0, \sqsupset, *_\circ \rangle_{\circ \in O}$, *the interpretation of formulas of Definition 3.2.2 is extended to* $\mathcal{L}^\sigma$ *by the following recursive clause:*

$$[\![\forall p\varphi]\!]_{\mathfrak{A},a} = \bigwedge_{x \in A} [\![\varphi]\!]_{\mathfrak{A},a[x/p]}$$

Again, this is a straightforward generalization of neighborhood frames, with neighborhood frames falling out as the special case of atomic CBAES. Furthermore, CBAES suffice to guarantee congruentiality, even in the presence of propositional quantifiers:

Proposition 3.2.4 *For any class* C *of* CBAES, $\mathcal{L}^\sigma(\mathsf{C})$ *is a* CPQML.

Proof The argument is routine except for the case of UG. For this case, we appeal to the following law of complete Boolean algebras: $\bigwedge_{y \in Y} x \sqsupset y = x \sqsupset \bigwedge Y$. This follows from the infinite distributivity laws of complete Boolean algebras; see (the dual of) Givant and Halmos (2009, p. 47, lemma 3). $\square$

Requiring algebras to be complete makes interpreting propositional quantifiers easy. But it breaks the simple and general completeness proofs for CMLS with respect to BAES: typically, Lindenbaum–Tarski algebras are incomplete, and it is not obvious how to complete them without affecting the interpretation of propositional quantifiers, as discussed by Holliday (2019). In fact, there are not just CPQMLS, but also NPQMLS which are incomplete with respect to the class of CBAES they define, and therefore not determined by any class of CBAES. It is worth noting that this does not straightforwardly follow from the fact, shown by Litak (2004), that there are NMLS which are not determined by any class of CBAES: recall from Proposition 2.3.9 that the extension of such an NML need not be conservative, and so need not itself fail to be determined by any class of of CBAES.

The existence of NPQMLS which are incomplete with respect to any class of CBAES can be shown using two results of Ding (2021a,b). First, Ding (2021b, p. 53, theorem 3.2.16) shows that there are instances of the following schema which are not derivable in $K_\Pi D45$:

$(4^\vee)$ $\forall p \Box \varphi \rightarrow \Box \forall p \Box \varphi$

(We return to the kinds of models used in this proof in Section 3.6.) Second, Ding (2021a, p. 1162, theorem 3.1) shows that all instances of $4^\vee$ are valid on the class of CBAES defined by $K_\Pi D45$. (Moreover, Ding (2021a) shows that $K_\Pi D4^\vee 5$ is sound and complete with respect to this class.) Therefore:

Proposition 3.2.5 $K_\Pi D45$ *is not the logic of any class of* CBAES.

Most of the existing work on CBAES is concerned with normal logics, despite the fact that CBAES constitute a natural model theory for the wider class of congruential logics. As in the case of neighborhood frames, BAES whose logic is normal have to satisfy certain constraints. In particular, since $\Box\top$ and $\Box(p \wedge q) \leftrightarrow (\Box p \wedge \Box q)$ are contained in every NML for every modality $\Box$, such BAEs must satisfy the following conditions, for every modality $\Box$:

(Normality) $*_\Box 1 = 1$

(Additivity) For all elements x and y, $*_\Box(x \sqcap y) = (*_\Box x \sqcap *_\Box y)$.

Conversely, these constraints suffice to guarantee normality, as the next proposition notes. (BAEs satisfying these constraints are often called "Boolean algebras with operators", for example, by Blackburn et al. (2001, p. 277). In the present context, this is confusing, since BAEs are literally Boolean algebras with arbitrary extra operators (functions), and so arguably most deserving of this label.)

Proposition 3.2.6 *A BAE $\mathfrak{A}$ for a unary modal signature O satisfies normality and additivity for every $\Box \in O$ if and only if the $\mathcal{L}_{qf}^O$-formulas valid on $\mathfrak{A}$ form an NML (in which case the $\mathcal{L}^O$-formulas valid on $\mathfrak{A}$ form an NPQML).*

Proof The left-to-right direction follows from the fact that if $\mathfrak{A}$ satisfies normality and additivity, then its validities contain $\Box\top$ (and so the $\mathcal{L}_{qf}^O$-formulas valid on $\mathfrak{A}$ are closed under necessitation), and the axiom $K_\Box$. The right-to-left direction follows from the fact that every NML contains $\Box\top$ and $\Box(p \wedge q) \leftrightarrow (\Box p \wedge \Box q)$. $\square$

In the context of CBAEs, it is natural to consider a generalization of additivity to arbitrary greatest lower bounds:

(Complete Additivity) For every set of elements X, $*_\Box \bigwedge X = \bigwedge\{*_\Box x : x \in X\}$.

In certain cases, this stronger condition leads to additional validities. This can be illustrated using results by Ding (2021a), who shows that $K_\Pi D4^\vee 5$ – which is complete with respect the class of CBAEs it defines – is incomplete if this class is restricted to CBAEs whose modal operation is completely additive. This is witnessed by certain instances of the Barcan formula. With Bc, $4^\vee$ becomes derivable; in fact, Ding shows:

Proposition 3.2.7 $K_\Pi D45Bc$ *is sound and complete with respect to a class of CBAEs whose modal function satisfies complete additivity.*

Ding also considers At, and shows that At becomes valid if, in addition to complete additivity, we restrict ourselves to *atomic* CBAES. Such CBAES are simply relational frames, algebraically presented. Consequently, Proposition 2.7.2 shows the soundness and completeness of $K_\Pi D45BcAt$ with respect to the class of such CBAEs it defines. Conversely, At can be falsified on nonatomic CBAEs, which shows that At is not derivable from $K_{\Pi}D45Bc$.

Corresponding results on At have been obtained in the stronger setting of S5, in which they take on an especially simple form. Recall from Section 2.5 that $S_{\Pi}5At$ is sound and complete with respect to the class of relational frames with a universal relation. Algebraically, a universal accessibility relation determines an operation $*_{\square}$ on the power set $\mathcal{P}(W)$ which maps 1 to itself, and every other proposition to 0. This treatment of $\square$ is straightforwardly extended to arbitrary BAEs, and it is easy to see that any such function $*_{\square}$ satisfies normality and complete additivity. Such algebras were already considered by Lewis and Langford (1959 [1932], p. 501), where they are attributed to Paul Henle. We therefore define:

Definition 3.2.8 *A Henle algebra is a* BAE $\langle A, 0, \sqsupset, *_{\square} \rangle$ *such that for all $x \in A$:*

$$*_{\square}(x) = \begin{cases} 1 & \text{if } x = 1 \\ 0 & \text{otherwise} \end{cases}$$

Complete and atomic Henle algebras are simply relational frames with a universal accessibility relation, algebraically presented. We therefore know from Theorem 2.5.1 that At is valid on such Henle algebras. In fact, we know that the logic of such Henle algebras is exactly $S_{\Pi}5At$. But what happens in nonatomic complete Henle algebras? Bull (1969, p. 260) observed that At is not valid on any complete Henle algebra which is not atomic. However, it is easy to see that the axioms T and 5 are valid on all complete Henle algebras, from which it follows that $S_{\Pi}5$ is sound with respect to complete Henle algebras. Along these lines, Bull concludes:

Proposition 3.2.9 At *is not a theorem of* $S_{\Pi}5$.

This result, together with the completeness of $S_{\Pi}5At$ with respect to complete atomic Henle algebras, suggests two very natural conjectures: first, that completeness is preserved when At is removed and nonatomic algebras are admitted, and second, that completeness is preserved when At is replaced by its negation ¬At, and only atomless algebras are considered. These very natural conjectures were only recently confirmed by Holliday (2019), who established the following companions to Theorem 2.5.1:

Proposition 3.2.10 $S_{\Pi}5$ *is sound and complete with respect to complete Henle algebras, and* $S_{\Pi}5\neg At$ *is sound and complete with respect to complete atomless Henle algebras.*

The results of Ding and Holliday concern two very strong NMLs, namely KD45 and S5. This is no accident, since the proof methods used by both authors heavily depend on the quantifier elimination technique of Kaplan (1970b) and Fine (1970). Fine had already extended these methods to $S_\Pi 5$, which he used to establish the decidability of this logic. These methods also allow Ding (2021a) to establish decidability for all of the particular extensions of $K_\Pi D45$ discussed by him. However, it is far from clear that these quantifier elimination results can be extended to weaker NMLs. Consequently, many open questions remain, many of which will likely require very different techniques. A basic example is the following:

Open Question 6 *Is the propositionally quantified modal logic of the class of all* CBAES *recursively enumerable?*

Depending on the answer to the this question, many variants and further questions arise. For example, if the answer to this question is positive, is E_Π complete with respect to the class of all CBAES? Is the answer the same if we consider unary modal signatures, and CBAES whose modal functions satisfy normality and (complete) additivity? Can the logic of such restricted classes of CBAES be completely axiomatized using K_Π? Are the answers to any of these questions dependent on the modal signature? For further discussion of open questions, see Holliday (2019) and Ding (2021a).

Before moving on to another topic, it is worth noting an alternative approach to CBAES. Recall how neighborhood frames can be considered as the special case of *atomic* CBAES. (Similarly, relational frames can be considered as the special case of *atomic* CBAES with modal functions satisfying normality and complete additivity.) This follows from Proposition 3.2.1, which in algebraic terminology is a representation theorem, showing that complete *atomic* Boolean algebras can be represented using powerset algebras. There is a more general representation theorem, which shows that *all* complete Boolean algebras can be represented as the completions of arbitrary partial orders, or, equivalently, as the *regular open subalgebras* of arbitrary topological spaces. The former representation theorem is often attributed to Tarski (1935), and the latter to Tarski (1937) and MacNeille (1937).

In the representation of complete Boolean algebras using partial orders, the elements of the order can be understood as (possibly incomplete) possibilities, and so as a generalization of the concept of possible worlds. Furthermore, the evaluation of formulas can be formulated in terms of being made true by a possibility, and even the accessibility relations of relational frames can be applied to possibilities to interpret unary modal operators when considering algebras whose modal functions satisfy normality and additivity. (Along with neighborhood frames, these models therefore exemplify the earlier claim that the model-theoretic ideas of possible worlds and accessibility relations are entirely separable.) Such a possibility semantics for propositional modal languages was proposed by Humberstone (1981); the general theory and connection to algebraic models is developed in detail by Holliday (forthcoming). These models can be extended to provide an elegant model theory for propositionally quantified modal logic; see Holliday (2021, section 5.1) for an illustration.

3.3 Pointed Frames, and Matrices

There is one more way in which we can generalize the model theories and modal logics we have considered so far. Consider first again the simplest case of unimodal relational frames; we return to BAEs in a moment. In such frames, worlds play two roles: First, and most obviously, the worlds accessible from a given world play the role of representing the ways things *could* be (according to the modality under consideration, from the perspective of the given world). For example, if $\Box$ is interpreted as being known by a particular agent, the worlds accessible from the world of evaluation represent the ways things could be, given the agent's knowledge at the given world. But worlds also play a second role, which is to represent the way things could logically be. In the example just mentioned, a frame might contain a world which can only access itself, as well as a world which can access itself as well as another world. As a consequence, the logic of the frame allows both for the agent to be omniscient, as well as for them not to be omniscient, in the sense that neither $\forall p(p \rightarrow \Box p)$ nor its negation is included in the logic of the frame.

These two roles played by worlds are already partly separated in relational frames by the accessibility relation, since not every world is possible (from the perspective of a given world) according to the standard of the relevant object-language modality. But in relational frames, *every* world must serve to constrain the logic, since validity is defined as truth in all worlds of the frame (under every assignment function). In this sense, all worlds of relational frames are logically possible worlds. It is therefore impossible to use worlds to constrain the behaviour of modal operators without also constraining the logic. For example, if we want to represent an agent not knowing that knowledge is factive, that is, if we want a world to verify the principle $\neg\Box\forall p(\Box p \rightarrow p)$, we have to admit a world which is not accessible from itself. But this means that the factivity of knowledge, $\forall p(\Box p \rightarrow p)$, will not be included in the logic of the frame. More abstractly, the requirement for all worlds of a frame to count as logically possible worlds forces logics of relational frames to be closed under necessitation.

However, these limitations are easily overcome: In a given frame, we can *distinguish* certain worlds as logically possible, simply by including in the definition of a frame a subset of worlds which are to count as logically possible. Then we can, for example, consider a class of frames with distinguished worlds in which every distinguished world can access itself, without imposing the same requirement on all worlds. On the resulting class of frames, $\forall p(\Box p \rightarrow p)$ is valid, without $\Box \forall p(\Box p \rightarrow p)$ thereby becoming valid as well. This separation of the two roles of possible worlds was in fact present in the original definition of relational frames of Kripke (1963a). Kripke requires there to be just a single distinguished world, but this choice is easily seen to be immaterial when we consider logics of classes of frames: The logic of any class C of frames with a set of distinguished worlds is the same as the logic of the class of frames obtained from frames in C by restricting the set of distinguished worlds to a singleton. Here we follow Kripke and distinguish a single world. We call the resulting frames *pointed*.

The addition of a distinguished world extends straightforwardly to the case of neighborhood frames. For brevity, we introduce pointed relational and neighborhood frames together:

Definition 3.3.1 *A pointed relational/neighborhood frame is a structure* $\mathfrak{F} =$ $\langle W, w_0, X_o \rangle_{o \in O}$ *such that* $\langle W, X_o \rangle_{o \in O}$ *is a relational/neighborhood frame, and* $w_0 \in W$. *Assignment functions and truth are defined as in Definition 2.3.1/3.1.1. Validity on a frame is defined as follows:*

$$\mathfrak{F} \Vdash \varphi \text{ if } \mathfrak{F}, w_0, a \Vdash \varphi \text{ for all } a: \Phi \rightarrow \mathcal{P}(W).$$

What kind of logics do we get from classes of pointed frames? We have already seen that in the relational case, they need not be normal, as they need not be closed under necessitation. Similarly, in the neighborhood case, they need not be congruential. However, the logic of any class of pointed relational/neighborhood frame must *include some* normal/congruential modal logic, namely the logic of the class of relational/neighborhood frames which we get from omitting the distinguished worlds. Consequently, the logic of any class of pointed frames must contain the smallest normal/congruential logic. The logic of any class of pointed frames must also be classical. These two constraints lead to the following definition:

Definition 3.3.2 *A set* $\Lambda \subseteq \mathcal{L}^\sigma$ *is a quasi-normal/quasi-congruential (propositionally quantified) modal logic if it is a classical (propositionally quantified) modal logic including some normal/congruential (propositionally quantified) modal logic.*

We abbreviate "quasi-normal/quasi-congruential (propositionally quantified) modal logic" as "QNML/QCML(QNPQML/QCPQML)". As discussed by Segerberg (1971), classes of pointed relational/neighborhood frames give us QNMLS/QCMLS, and we now note that the analogous claim holds in the presence of propositional quantifiers:

Proposition 3.3.3 *For any class of pointed relational/neighborhood frames* C, $\mathcal{L}^{\sigma}(C)$ *is a* QNPQML/QCPQML.

Proof That $\mathcal{L}^{\sigma}(C)$ includes an NPQML/CPQML follows from Propositions 2.3.4 and 3.1.3. Classicality is routine, considering each of the four conditions. □

Pointed frames are often not considered since many of the formal results on relational and neighborhood frames transfer straightforwardly to pointed frames. But there are many applications of modal logics in which the additional flexibility of pointed frames is important. An example from philosophy is the logic of indexical operators, such as "now" and "actually", investigated by Kaplan (1989 [1977]) and Crossley and Humberstone (1977). An example from mathematics is the QNML GLS, which Solovay (1976) showed to capture the notion of provability from the axioms of Peano arithmetic according to true arithmetic, on the provability interpretation of modal logic; this is discussed in more detail in Boolos (1985). In the context of neighborhood frames, pointed frames also allow the construction of model theories of some lesser known Lewis systems, including S2 and S3, since the models of Kripke (1965) for these systems can be formulated as pointed neighborhood frames.

In many cases, the problem of the axiomatizability of a propositionally quantified modal logic of a class of pointed frames can be reduced to the known problem of the axiomatizability of the logic of a corresponding class of unpointed frames. Exemplarily, we consider the case of (any class of) pointed relational frames in which for some fixed modality $\Box$, $R_{\Box}$ is universal. First, let O be a unary modal signature, and define O' to be the signature obtained from O by adding one further unary operator $\triangle$. For any pointed relational frame $\mathfrak{F}$ for σ, let $\mathfrak{F}'$ be the relational frame for σ' obtained by removing the distinguished world w_0 from $\mathfrak{F}$ and adding an accessibility relation $R_{\triangle}$ such that, in general, wR_0v if and only if $v = w_0$. We show that there are simple recursive mappings which reduce the logics of $\mathfrak{F}'$ and $\mathfrak{F}$ to each other. One direction is straightforward, as any formula $\varphi \in \mathcal{L}^{\sigma}$ is valid on $\mathfrak{F}$ just in case $\triangle\varphi$ is valid on $\mathfrak{F}'$. For the converse direction, define φ' for every $\varphi \in \mathcal{L}^{\sigma}$ recursively using the single nontrivial clause $(\triangle\varphi)' := \Box(p_0 \to \varphi')$, where we assume that p_0 does not already occur in any formula φ under consideration. We can now show that

$\varphi \in \mathcal{L}^{\sigma'}$ is valid on $\mathfrak{F}'$ just in case $\forall p_0(Q(p_0) \wedge p_0 \rightarrow \Box\varphi')$ is valid on $\mathfrak{F}$, where Q is used as defined in Section 2.4.

Consider now the case of BAEs. Recall that BAEs can be understood as generalizing neighborhood frames by dropping the requirement of the (implicit) underlying Boolean algebra to be complete and atomic. Such algebraic structures therefore need not contain atoms, which would correspond to possible worlds. We can therefore not easily adapt the idea of distinguishing a single world. But as noted earlier, instead of pointed frames we can also work with frames with sets of distinguished elements. Sets of worlds correspond to elements of a Boolean algebra, so we can extend frames with distinguished elements to BAEs by distinguishing one element x_0 of the algebra. Validity is then defined by letting a formula φ be valid just in case its interpretation is entailed (according to the Boolean order $\leq$) by x_0, under every assignment function.

The distinguished element x_0 determines the set of propositions $\uparrow x_0$ it entails. A formula is then valid just in case, for every assignment function, it is interpreted as a member of this set. By construction, $\uparrow x_0$ is guaranteed to be a filter, where the notion of a filter is generalized to arbitrary Boolean algebras as follows: $F \subseteq A$ is a *filter* of $\langle A, 0, \sqsupset \rangle$ if $1 \in F$, $x \sqcap y \in F$ for any $x, y \in F$, and $x \sqcup y \in F$ for any $x \in F$, $y \in A$. This ensures that the quantifier-free validities form a classical modal logic. In fact, $\uparrow x_0$ is by definition a *principal filter*, which means that it is not just closed under binary greatest lower bounds, but arbitrary greatest lower bounds: $\bigwedge X \in \uparrow x_0$ for all $X \subseteq \uparrow x_0$. In the quantifier-free case, this additional requirement is not needed to ensure that the resulting logic is classical. So, in the quantifier-free case, the notion of a pointed neighborhood frame can be generalized to the notion of a BAE extended by a filter F, where a formula counts as valid just in case its interpretation is a member of F, under every assignment function. This leads us to the notion of a *matrix*, which goes back to the very beginnings of work in symbolic logic, as noted by Łukasiewicz and Tarski (1930). In the context of modal logics, matrices were used as early as McKinsey (1941).

Definition 3.3.4 *A* (C)BAE-matrix *is a structure* $\mathfrak{M} = \langle A, 0, \sqsupset, F, *_\circ \rangle_{\circ \in O}$ *such that* $\langle A, 0, \sqsupset, *_\circ \rangle_{\circ \in O}$ *is a* (C)BAE, *and F is a filter of* $\langle A, 0, \sqsupset \rangle$. *Assignment functions and evaluation are defined as in Definition 3.2.2. Validity on a matrix is defined as follows:*

$\mathfrak{A} \Vdash \varphi$ *if and only if* $[\![\varphi]\!]_{\mathfrak{A},a} \in F$.

From this definition, it is easy to see that the notion of a BAE can be understood as the special case of a BAE-matrix with the singleton filter $\{1\}$.

The logic of any class of BAE-matrices is a QCML. In fact, as in the case of BAES and CMLS, the logics of classes of BAE-matrices are all and only the QCMLS; see Hansson and Gärdenfors (1973). Turning to propositionally quantified logics, we restrict ourselves to CBAES as in the previous section, to guarantee that greatest lower bounds are always defined. This does not suffice, however, to ensure classicality, as we now demonstrate. The proof employs the notion of an *ultrafilter*, which is a filter which contains, for every element x, either x or $-x$, but not both.

Proposition 3.3.5 *There is a* CBAE-*matrix* $\mathfrak{M}$ *for the unary unimodal signature such that* $\mathcal{L}^{\square}(\mathfrak{M})$ *is not classical.*

Proof Let $\langle A, 0, \beth \rangle$ be an infinite complete Boolean algebra, and U a nonprincipal ultrafilter. (Using the axiom of choice, it can be shown that there must be such a filter.) Define $*_{\square} : A \to A$ such that for all $x \in A$:

$$*_{\square}(x) = \begin{cases} x & \text{if } x \in U \\ -x & \text{otherwise} \end{cases}$$

Let $\mathfrak{M} = \langle A, 0, \beth, U, *_{\square} \rangle$. Then $\mathcal{L}^{\square}(\mathfrak{M})$ does not satisfy UG, since $\mathfrak{M} \Vdash \square p$, but $\mathfrak{M} \nVdash \forall p \square p$. $\qquad \square$

The problem can be overcome by requiring the filters of CBAE-matrices to be principal:

Proposition 3.3.6 *For any class* C *of* CBAE-*matrices with principal filters,* $\mathcal{L}^{\sigma}(C)$ *is a* QCPQML.

Proof The crucial case of UG is as in the proof of Proposition 3.2.4, using the fact that principal filters are closed under arbitrary greatest lower bounds. $\qquad \square$

Along the lines of Proposition 3.2.6, it is easy to conclude from this that if the modal functions of a class of CBAE-matrices with principal filters satisfy normality and additivity, the logic of the class is a QNPQML.

3.4 Incomplete Boolean Algebras

So far, we have only interpreted propositional quantifiers on *complete* BAES. Completeness immediately guarantees that universal propositional quantifiers can be interpreted as greatest lower bounds, since *every* set has a greatest lower bound. But we really only need a weaker condition, which is that greatest lower bounds exist for sets of propositions determined by open formulas. That is, we need that for every formula φ, variable p, and assignment function a, the set of elements $[\![\varphi]\!]_{a[x/p]}$, for arbitrary elements x, has a greatest lower bound. This motivates the following definition:

Definition 3.4.1 *A* BAE $\mathfrak{A} = \langle A, 0, \sqsupset, *_\circ \rangle_{\circ \in O}$ *is* quantifiable *if there is a function* $[\![\cdot]\!]$. *which satisfies the evaluation conditions of Definitions 3.2.2 and 3.2.3. If so, validity is defined as in Definition 3.2.2.*

We call quantifiable BAES QBAES. A simple way of demonstrating that QBAES need not be complete considers the nonmodal case, that is, the limiting case of the empty modal signature. In this case, it can be shown that *every* Boolean algebra $\mathfrak{A} = \langle A, 0, \sqsupset \rangle$ is quantifiable. This follows along the lines of the elimination of propositional quantifiers in Section 1.3: it can be shown that $[\![\varphi]\!]_{\mathfrak{A},a[1/p]} \sqcap [\![\varphi]\!]_{\mathfrak{A},a[0/p]}$ is always the greatest lower bound of $\{[\![\varphi]\!]_{\mathfrak{A},a[x/p]} : x \in A\}$, whence the latter always exists. We will see more interesting examples in a moment, in connection with Proposition 3.4.3.

Naturally, not every BAE is quantifiable. For a simple example, add to the algebra of finite and cofinite subsets of $\mathbb{N}$ a bijection $*_\square$ from the algebra to the set of singletons of even numbers. Then the interpretation of $\forall p \square p$ requires the set of singletons of even numbers to have a greatest lower bound, which does not exist. However, on such non-quantifiable BAES, one can at least interpret the combined modal-quantificational propositional quantifier $[\forall p]$ investigated by Holliday and Litak (2018), whose interpretation is given by the following condition:

$$[\![[\forall p]\varphi]\!]_{\mathfrak{A},a} = \begin{cases} 1 & \text{if } [\![\varphi]\!]_{\mathfrak{A},a[x/p]} = 1 \text{ for all } x \in A \\ 0 & \text{otherwise} \end{cases}$$

Returning to quantifiable BAES, we note that their restrictions suffice to ensure congruentiality:

Proposition 3.4.2 *For any class* C *of* QBAES, $\mathcal{L}^\sigma(\mathsf{C})$ *is a* CPQML.

Proof A straightforward generalization of Proposition 3.2.4, using the fact that the relevant infinite distributive law holds in all Boolean algebra, whenever the relevant greatest lower bounds are defined.   □

Furthermore, the constraints on QBAES are weak enough to allow us to prove also that *every* CPQML is the logic of a class of QBAES. QBAES therefore stand to CPQMLS as BAES stand to CMLS: the logics of QBAES are all and only the CPQMLS. In particular, every CPQML is (sound and) complete with respect to the class of QBAES it defines.

Proposition 3.4.3 *Any* CPQML *is* $\mathcal{L}^\sigma(\mathsf{C})$ *for some class* C *of* QBAEs.

Proof Via a standard construction of a Lindenbaum–Tarski algebra, using the fact that in any CPQML, provable equivalence is a congruence with respect to the Boolean and modal connectives, and formulas which are alphabetical variants in bound variables are provably equivalent. □

With Proposition 3.2.6, we get as an immediate corollary the same claim for NPQMLs and QBAEs satisfying normality and additivity:

Corollary 3.4.4 *Any* NPQML *is* $\mathcal{L}^\sigma(\mathsf{C})$ *for some class* C *of* QBAEs *satisfying normality and additivity.*

As further immediate corollaries, we get that E_Π is the propositionally quantified modal logic of the class of all QBAEs, and K_Π is the propositionally quantified modal logic of the class of all QBAEs which satisfy normality and additivity. It is also worth noting that the QBAEs used in the proof of Proposition 3.4.3 are all based on a countable atomless Boolean algebra, which is unique up to isomorphism, and incomplete. This provides us with many more examples of BAEs which are incomplete but nevertheless quantifiable.

3.5 General Frames

We saw earlier that neighborhood frames can be thought of as concrete representations of complete and atomic BAEs. In the context of propositional modal logics without quantifiers, there is a straightforward way of generalizing the definition of these frames so that they serve as concrete representations of all BAEs. The resulting structures are known as *general frames*. As the name suggests, they bear a certain correspondence to the general models for higher-order logic of Henkin (1950). In the context of propositional modal logics without quantifiers, they were first used by Thomason (1972). As Thomason notes, it is interesting that in the context of propositionally quantified modal logics, they were already used slightly earlier, by Bull (1969) and Fine (1970). In this context, the notion of a general frame arises in two subtly different forms. We start with the quantifier-free case.

By a famous representation theorem of Stone (1936), every Boolean algebra is isomorphic to a *field of sets*, that is, a subset of a power set which is closed under finite set-theoretic operations (e.g., intersection and relative complement). With this representation theorem, the concrete representation of complete and atomic BAEs using neighborhood frames can be extended to arbitrary BAEs by adjoining to the frame a field of sets A. Effectively, we can think of A as delimiting which sets of possible worlds are to count as propositions. We only need to ensure that every formula expresses a proposition in A, under every assignment function whose image is included in A (which also guarantees that A is a field of sets). The definition extends straightforwardly to relational frames, so we define the two concepts together:

Definition 3.5.1 *A general relational/neighborhood frame (for a modal signature $\sigma = \langle O, \rho \rangle$) is a structure $\mathfrak{F} = \langle W, A, X_\circ \rangle_{\circ \in O}$ such that $\langle W, X_\circ \rangle_{\circ \in O}$ is a relational/neighborhood frame and $A \subseteq \mathcal{P}(W)$, such that $[\![\varphi]\!]_{\mathfrak{F},a} \in A$ for every formula $\varphi \in \mathcal{L}_{\mathrm{qf}}^\sigma$ and $a\colon \Phi \to A$, on the standard truth-conditional interpretation of $[\![\cdot]\!]$. given by Definitions 2.3.1 and 3.1.1. Validity is defined by letting $\mathfrak{F} \Vdash \varphi$ if $\mathfrak{F}, w, a \Vdash \varphi$ for all $w \in W$ and $a\colon \Phi \to A$.*

In the case of general relational frames, the connection to BAES whose modal functions satisfy normality and additivity can also be spelled out algebraically, using a generalization of Stone's representation theorem due to Jónnson and Tarski (1951, 1952). The correspondences between general relational/neighborhood frames and the relevant classes of BAES have been investigated in great generality using the tools of category theory; see Thomason (1975) and Došen (1989).

By Stone's representation theorem, general neighborhood frames and BAES behave exactly alike as models of CMLS. First, every general neighborhood frame $\mathfrak{F} = \langle W, A, N_\circ \rangle_{\circ \in O}$ corresponds to some BAE based on the field of sets A, with $*$ derived from N as discussed in Section 3.2. Conversely, since any Boolean algebra is isomorphic to some field of sets $A \subseteq \mathcal{P}(W)$, any BAE $\mathfrak{B}$ based on this Boolean algebra corresponds to a general neighborhood frame $\mathfrak{F}$ based on W and A. Furthermore, the evaluation of quantifier-free formula is preserved by the correspondence, in the sense that for any isomorphism f from A to $\mathfrak{B}$, assignment function $a\colon \Phi \to A$, and $\varphi \in \mathcal{L}_{\mathrm{qf}}, f([\![\varphi]\!]_{\mathfrak{F},a}) = [\![\varphi]\!]_{\mathfrak{B},f \circ a}$. General frames therefore add only mathematical convenience in the presentation of BAES.

The situation changes when we add propositional quantifiers. For example, consider a CBAE $\mathfrak{A}$, and a corresponding general neighborhood frame $\mathfrak{F}$. When interpreting propositional quantifiers on $\mathfrak{F} = \langle W, A, N_\circ \rangle_{\circ \in O}$, we might naturally employ the standard truth-conditions of quantifiers, restricted to the designated algebra of propositions:

$$\mathfrak{F}, w, a \Vdash \forall p\varphi \text{ if and only if } \mathfrak{F}, w, a[x/p] \Vdash \varphi \text{ for all } x \in A.$$

Along the lines discussed in Section 3.2, this means that the evaluation clause for propositional quantifiers is the following:

$[\![\forall p \varphi]\!]_{\mathfrak{F},a} = \bigcap_{x \in A} [\![\varphi]\!]_{\mathfrak{F},a[x/p]}$

But note that the evaluation clause on the algebraic side interprets propositional quantifiers using greatest lower bounds. Transferring this condition to the setting of general frames, we obtain the following condition:

$[\![\forall p \varphi]\!]_{\mathfrak{F},a} = \bigwedge_{x \in A} [\![\varphi]\!]_{\mathfrak{F},a[x/p]}$

When considering a (standard) neighborhood frame as a BAE, the underlying Boolean algebra is a power set algebra, in which greatest lower bounds are always intersections. But in arbitrary fields of sets, greatest lower bounds may come apart from intersections. This means that for general neighborhood frames, the two evaluation conditions for propositional quantifiers may come apart. In the presence of propositional quantifiers, there are therefore two natural conceptions of general frames. (We will shortly see concrete examples where they come apart.)

The notion of general frames on which propositional quantifiers are evaluated using greatest lower bounds is simply a concrete representation of the notion of a BAE, where we will have to restrict ourselves to frames corresponding to QBAES in order for propositional quantifiers to be interpretable. The resulting model theory can be seen as a propositionally quantified modal version of the (constant domain version of the) admissibility semantics developed for propositionally quantified relevant logics by Goldblatt and Kane (2010) and for modal predicate logics by Goldblatt (2011). In contrast, the conception of general frames on which propositional quantifiers are given the standard truth-conditional interpretation leads to a class of models which come apart from QBAES, so we consider these for the remainder of this section. These were also the models investigated by Bull (1969) and Fine (1970).

Definition 3.5.2 *A general relational/neighborhood frame* $\mathfrak{F} = \langle W, A, X_\circ \rangle_{\circ \in O}$ *is* quantifiable *if* $[\![\varphi]\!]_{\mathfrak{F},a} \in A$ *for every formula* $\varphi \in \mathcal{L}^\sigma$ *and* $a \colon \Phi \to A$, *where Definition 3.5.1 is extended to quantified formulas using the following clause:*

$\mathfrak{F}, w, a \Vdash \forall p \varphi$ *if and only if* $\mathfrak{F}, w, a[x/p] \Vdash \varphi$ *for all* $x \in A$.

We abbreviate "quantifiable general relational/neighborhood frame" as "QGRF"/"QGNF".

In the quantifier-free case, general frames are easy to construct: We can start with any set of sets $X \subseteq \mathcal{P}(W)$ and accessibility relations or neighborhood functions on W. Since we can think of the various connectives of $\mathcal{L}_{qf}$ as interpreted using operators on $\mathcal{P}(W)$, we can simply close X under these operators, that is, we can take the smallest subset $A \subseteq \mathcal{P}(W)$ closed under these operators.

The same is not possible for quantifiers: The interpretation of a quantified formula depends on the domain of quantification, namely, the very field of sets we are trying to construct. Consequently, we cannot construct a quantifiable general frame simply by starting from any set and closing it to include all the "required" propositions: which propositions are required depends on the algebra of propositions, which is just being determined.

How do QGNFs relate to QBAES? It is easy to see that if a general neighborhood frame is quantifiable, then the BAE to which it corresponds is quantifiable as well. This follows from the fact that for any field of sets A and $X \subseteq A$, if $\bigcap X \in A$, then $\bigcap X$ is the greatest lower bound of X in A. This is a useful observation since it allows us to construct further examples of BAEs which are quantifiable without being complete: Recall that the examples of such BAEs arising from Proposition 3.4.3 are all atomless. In contrast, many useful examples of general relational and neighborhood frames are based on incomplete atomic fields of sets, and some of them are easily shown to be quantifiable. The QGRF $\mathfrak{S}$ defined in the following discussion is an example.

Every QGNF corresponds to a QBAE, but the converse is not the case. Indeed, there is a CBAE which does not correspond to any QGNF. Let $\mathfrak{A}$ be a BAE for the unary unimodal signature based on a complete atomless field of sets $A \subseteq \mathcal{P}(W)$, with a function $*_\Box$ defined as in the proof of Proposition 3.3.5, where $U = \{x \in A : a \in x\}$ for some $a \in W$. (Since A is atomless, U is a nonprincipal ultrafilter.) Let $\mathfrak{F}$ be the general neighborhood frame corresponding to $\mathfrak{A}$, based on W and A. Then $\bigcap\{[\![\Box p]\!]_{\mathfrak{F},a[x/p]} : x \in A\}$ is $\{a\}$. Since A is atomless, $\{a\} \notin A$. Thus, $\mathfrak{F}$ is not quantifiable: the intersection needed to interpret $\forall p \Box p$ is not an element of the underlying field of sets.

QGNFs can therefore be seen as a properly special case of QBAES, and analogously for QGRFs and QBAEs satisfying normality additivity. It follows that quantifiable general frames guarantee the relevant deductive principles:

Proposition 3.5.3 *For any class* C *of* QGRF/QGNF, $\mathcal{L}^\sigma(C)$ *is an* NPQML/CPQML.

Proof Routine except for the case of UI, which follows using the fact that $[\![\varphi]\!]_{\mathfrak{F},a}$ is guaranteed to be a member of A. $\qquad\qquad\square$

General frames have mostly been considered in the form of general relational frames. It is easy to see that all instances of the Barcan formula Bc are valid on QGRFs. In contrast, At is not valid on all QGRFs. This follows from the following completeness results of Bull (1969) (the last two) and Fine (1970), together with Proposition 3.2.9 on the underivability of At:

Theorem 3.5.4 $K_\Pi Bc$, $K_\Pi TBc$, $S_\Pi 4Bc$ *and* $S_\Pi 5$ *are complete with respect to the classes of* QGRFs *they define.*

The enumerative nature of this result immediately suggests the question whether it can be extended to all NPQMLs containing (every instance of) Bc. That is, is every NPQML containing Bc complete with respect to the class of QGRFs it defines, and so sound and complete with respect to some class of QGRFs? In unpublished work, Yipu Li and Yifeng Ding (pc) show that this is indeed the case.

For the four logics mentioned in Theorem 3.5.4, Fine also asserts a stronger claim: For any unimodal NML Λ, Fine defines $\Lambda\pi$ as the set of $\mathcal{L}^\square$-formulas valid on the class of QGRF *based on frames which validate* Λ. He then asserts that $K_\Pi Bc$ is $K\pi$, and similarly for the other three logics. He states that this can be proven using the canonical model technique. Furthermore, he asserts that these four logics are undecidable.

Fine's announcement of these results are noteworthy for two reasons. First, the completeness claims are genuinely stronger than Theorem 3.5.4, as there are cases in which the QGRFs based on frames validating a certain set of quantifier-free axioms Γ validate a quantified principle which is not validated on the bigger class of QGRFs which validate Γ. We show this in Proposition 3.5.6.

Second, Fine announces an even stronger completeness result, which is the corresponding completeness result for every NML which is canonical, where being *canonical* means being valid on its canonical frame. This claim can be understood in two ways, depending on which canonical frame is intended. On the one hand, since we are interested in the claim that $\Lambda\pi$ is $K_\Pi\Lambda Bc$, we might understand an NML Λ to be canonical if it is valid on the canonical frame for $K_\Pi\Lambda Bc$. On this understanding of canonicity, Fine's claim is confirmed by the work of Li and Ding. On the other hand, an NML Λ is normally understood to be canonical just in case it is valid on its own canonical frame, that is, the canonical frame for Λ. Fine's claim is false on this second way of understanding it. We show this in Proposition 3.5.7.

Both of these observations on Fine's results can be established using the same model construction, to which we now turn. We will also use it to complete the proof of Proposition 2.7.3; as noted there, the construction adapts the proof strategy of an incompleteness result in modal predicate logic.

Let $\mathfrak{S}$ be the general relational frame $\langle \mathbb{N}, S, \leq \rangle$, where S is the set of finite and cofinite subsets of $\mathbb{N}$. Equivalently, $x \in S$ if and only if there is some $n \in \mathbb{N}$ such that for all $m > n$, $m \in x$ if and only if $n \in x$. We can think of the members of S as the propositions whose truth-value *settles* at some world n, in the sense of staying the same in every world accessible from n.

Lemma 3.5.5 $\mathfrak{S}$ *is a* QGRF *validating* S4M.

Proof To show that $\mathfrak{S}$ is a QGRF, we need to show that, in general, $[\![\varphi]\!]_{\mathfrak{S},a} \in S$. This follows from the fact that whenever $a(p)$ is settled at n, for every variable p free in φ, $[\![\varphi]\!]_{\mathfrak{S},a}$ is settled at n, which can be shown by an induction on the complexity of φ. Only the case of quantifiers is interesting, which follows from the uniform structure of the frame. (This can be shown more rigorously using a version of the notion of generated subframes – stated in Definition 2.8.1 – for general frames. For further details, see Fritz (unpublished).)

Recall that S4M strengthens S4 by the McKinsey axiom M, which is $\Box\Diamond p \rightarrow \Diamond\Box p$. The validity of S4 is immediate since $\leq$ is reflexive and transitive. For M, note that $\mathfrak{S}, n, a \Vdash \Box\Diamond p$ requires $a(p)$ to settle to being true, which guarantees the truth of $\Diamond\Box p$. $\qquad\square$

We can now establish our first claim, that requiring the *underlying* frame to validate certain principles can be more demanding than requiring the general frame itself to validate these principles, and that this can be reflected in the validities on the relevant class of structures:

Proposition 3.5.6 $\Diamond\forall p(p \rightarrow \Box p)$ *is valid on every* QGRF *which is based on a frame validating S4M, but not on every* QGRF *which validates S4M.*

Proof A routine argument shows that in every relational frame validating S4M, every world w can access a world v such that $R_\Box(v) = \{v\}$; this ensures the validity of $\Diamond\forall p(p \rightarrow \Box p)$. However, $\mathfrak{S}$, which we have just shown to validate S4M, does not validate $\Diamond\forall p(p \rightarrow \Box p)$, since it contains no world at which all propositions are settled. $\qquad\square$

Next, we can show that the second reading of Fine's claim concerning canonical NMLS is incorrect:

Proposition 3.5.7 S4M *is a canonical* NML, *but* S4Mπ *is not completely axiomatized by* $S_\Pi 4MBc$ *(i.e.,* $K_\Pi T4MBc$*).*

Proof S4M is known to be canonical; see Hughes and Cresswell (1996, pp. 131–134). (This does not contradict the fact that the M axiom alone is *not* canonical, which was shown by Goldblatt (1991).) As shown in the proof of Proposition 3.5.6, $\Diamond\forall p(p \rightarrow \Box p)$ is a member of S4Mπ, but not valid on $\mathfrak{S}$. Since $\mathfrak{S}$ validates S4M, it validates $S_\Pi 4MBc$, whence $\Diamond\forall p(p \rightarrow \Box p)$ is not a theorem of $S_\Pi 4MBc$. So, $S_\Pi 4MBc$ does not completely axiomatize S4Mπ. $\qquad\square$

We can also use $\mathfrak{S}$ to prove an assertion used in the proof of Proposition 2.7.3:

Proposition 3.5.8 $K_\Pi 3.1BcAt$ *(i.e.,* $K_\Pi T4Lem_0J1BcAt)$ *does not prove* $\Diamond \forall p(p \to \Box p)$.

Proof Given the preceding results, it suffices to show that $K_\Pi 3.1BcAt$ is valid on $\mathfrak{S}$. The only interesting case is J1, that is, the formula $\Box(\Box(p \to \Box p) \to p) \to p$. Arguing contrapositively, consider any world n in which p is false, on a given variable assignment a. There are two options: either p is settled as false at some $m \geq n$, or p settles as true at $m + 1$ for some $m \geq n$ at which p is false. (For brevity, we conflate p and $a(p)$ in laying out the argument.) In both cases, it is easy to see that $\Box(p \to \Box p) \to p$ is false in m, whence $\Box(\Box(p \to \Box p) \to p)$ is false in n. Therefore J1 is valid on $\mathfrak{S}$. □

The requirement of being quantifiable ensures that general frames validate UI. But the interpretation of $\mathcal{L}^\sigma$ on general frames is well-defined without this requirement. In fact, we can even relax the requirement of general frames that $[\![\varphi]\!]_{\mathfrak{F},a}$ should be a member of the propositional domain, for every *quantifier-free* formula φ. Depending on how much this requirement is relaxed, the corresponding instances of UI might fail, so the relevant models will not in general lead to classical propositionally quantified modal logics. We therefore don't consider them in any detail here, but it should be noted that such wider classes of frames and correspondingly weaker logics were already considered by Fine (1970), who establishes certain completeness results for them as well. More recently, these results were extended by Belardinelli et al. (2018), who also consider the bimodal case. For a philosophical application of such weaker logics, see Bacon et al. (2016).

3.6 Variable Propositional Domains

So far, the frames we have considered effectively operate with a single propositional domain, over which propositional quantifiers range independently of the world of evaluation. However, there are applications where this feature is too restrictive. Consider the view that according to the notion of necessity operative in metaphysics, it is a contingent matter what things there are. Williamson (2013) calls this view *contingentism*, and the opposing view *necessitism*. Contingentism is attractive since it matches our pretheoretic judgements about simple cases such as the following: Ludwig Wittgenstein could have had a daughter. But since he actually had no children, there is plausibly nothing which could have been his daughter. So, there could have been something which does not actually exist, in the sense that actually, there is nothing identical to it. Conversely, Ludwig Wittgenstein could himself have failed to be born, in which case he would plausibly not have existed, in the sense that there would not have been anything identical to him. In this sense, then, there is something which might have failed to exist.

Some philosophers have not only endorsed contingentism, but also argued that propositions are existentially dependent on the individuals they are about; see, for example, Prior (1967), Fine (1977), Adams (1981), and Stalnaker (2012). For example, they would argue that the proposition that Ludwig Wittgenstein is a philosopher existentially depends on Ludwig Wittgenstein: had there not been Ludwig Wittgenstein, there would also not have been the proposition that Ludwig Wittgenstein is a philosopher. Similarly, had Ludwig Wittgenstein been the father of a daughter, the proposition that she is his daughter would have existed, but since she does not actually exist, neither does the proposition that she is his daughter. Adapting Williamson's terminology, Fritz (2016) calls the view that propositional existence is contingent *propositional contingentism*, and the opposing view *propositional necessitism*. Contingentism has therefore been argued to lead to propositional contingentism. This argument was already made by Prior, and Prior accommodated this propositional contingentism in his propositionally quantified modal logic; this led to his System Q in Prior (1957, chapter 5). Prior assumed that nonexistent propositions are neither true nor false, which led to a complicated and, from a modern perspective, unusual system. In the following, we will consider some less intrusive modifications to the models considered so far which nevertheless make room for propositional contingentism.

Prima facie, constructing models for propositional contingentism may seem relatively easy: one may simply enhance frames based on possible worlds by a form of the *variable domains* of Kripke (1963b). That is, we modify the general frames of the previous section by replacing the single domain of quantification A by a function D which maps every world to a domain of propositions over which the propositional quantifiers range at that world. One version of such a model theory was already proposed by Fine (1970, pp. 344–345). However, it is natural to require the propositional domains *at each world w* to be closed in very much the same sense as it was imposed on the domains of quantifiable general frames: any proposition expressed by a formula using parameters from the domain of w must itself be in the domain of w. (Here, a *parameter* is a proposition used as the interpretation of a free variable.) This requirement corresponds to a natural comprehension principle for propositional contingentism; see the principle discussed by Fritz (2017, p. 211), which is adapted from a corresponding principle of higher-order modal logic in Williamson (2013, p. 284). The definition of validity also requires some thought. In general frames, the

definition of validity considers only assignment functions which map propositional variables to elements in the propositional domain A. In variable domain
frames, the propositional domain is dependent on the world, so this requirement needs to be refined. One natural way of doing so defines φ to be valid on
a frame just in case φ is true in every world w under any assignment function
mapping every propositional variable to an element of the propositional domain
of w:

Definition 3.6.1 *A variable domain relational/neighborhood frame (for a modal
signature $\sigma = \langle O, \rho \rangle$) is a structure $\mathfrak{F} = \langle W, D, X_\circ \rangle_{\circ \in O}$ such that $\langle W, X_\circ \rangle_{\circ \in O}$ is
a relational/neighborhood frame and $D \colon W \to \mathcal{P}(\mathcal{P}(W))$, such that $[\![\varphi]\!]_{\mathfrak{F},a} \in
D(w)$ for every formula $\varphi \in \mathcal{L}^\sigma$, $w \in W$, and $a \colon \Phi \to D(w)$, on the stand-
ard truth-conditional interpretation of $[\![\cdot]\!]$. given by Definitions 2.3.1 and 3.1.1,
except for the following clause which is used for quantified formulas:*

$$\mathfrak{F}, w, a \Vdash \forall p \varphi \text{ if and only if } \mathfrak{F}, w, a[x/p] \Vdash \varphi \text{ for all } x \in D(w).$$

Validity is defined as follows:

$$\mathfrak{F} \Vdash \varphi \text{ if } \mathfrak{F}, w, a \Vdash \varphi \text{ for all } w \in W \text{ and } a \colon \Phi \to D(w).$$

In the following, we abbreviate "variable domain relational/neighborhood
frame" as "VDRF"/"VDNF". We can confirm that these model-theoretic constructions suffice to ensure classicality. Since VDRFs are effectively special cases of
VDNFs, it suffices to consider the following claim:

Proposition 3.6.2 *For any class C of VDNFs, $\mathcal{L}^\sigma(\mathsf{C})$ is a classical propositionally quantified modal logic.*

Proof Routine. For the validity of UI, we use the fact that $[\![\varphi]\!]_{\mathfrak{F},a} \in D(w)$ for
every formula $\varphi \in \mathcal{L}^\sigma$, $w \in W$, and $a \colon \Phi \to D(w)$. $\qquad \square$

VDNFs generalize QGNFs in a natural way, and many of the remarks on
QGNFs made in the previous section apply here as well. For example, the truth-
conditional interpretation of quantifiers could be replaced by an algebraic one,
and the resulting models would constitute a natural version of the admissibility semantics of Goldblatt (2011) for propositionally quantified modal logics.
Likewise, as in the case of quantifiable general frames, one cannot construct
variable domain frames just by starting with a stock of propositions assigned
to each world and then closing under definability in $\mathcal{L}^\sigma$; again, a stable interpretation of quantified formulas requires a fixed domain (function). It is therefore

useful to consider a more specific construction, with which a range of nontrivial variable domain frames can be defined.

The construction we will consider is based on work of Fine (1977) and Stalnaker (2012), and developed in Fritz (2017). It builds on the very simple case of relational frames with a universal accessibility relation. To determine propositional domains, one starts with an *equivalence system*, which is a function $\approx$ which associates each world w with an equivalence relation $\approx_w$ among worlds. Informally, $v \approx_w u$ is interpreted as v and u being indistinguishable from the perspective of w. A domain function D is then derived by letting $D(w)$ contain just those propositions which do not distinguish between indistinguishable worlds. This determines a VDRF as long as $\approx$ satisfies a certain condition of "quasicoherence", stated in the following definition. The condition makes use of the notion of an *automorphism* of an equivalence system $\approx$; this is a function f on the set of worlds such that for all worlds w, v, and u: $v \approx_w u$ if and only if $f(v) \approx_{f(w)} f(u)$.

Definition 3.6.3 *An* equivalence system *on a set W is a function $\approx$ mapping every $w \in W$ to an equivalence relation $\approx_w$.*

$\approx$ *is* quasicoherent *if for all $w, v, u \in W$ such that $v \approx_w u$, there is an automorphism f of $\approx$ such that $f(v) = u$ and $f \subseteq \approx_w$.*

$\mathfrak{F}_\approx$ *is the structure $\langle W, D, R \rangle$ such that $R = W \times W$, and D is the function mapping every $w \in W$ to:*

$$D(w) = \{x \subseteq W : if\, v \approx_w u,\, then\, v \in x \,if\, and\, only\, if\, u \in x\}$$

As the term "quasicoherent" indicates, there is a somewhat stronger condition of being *coherent*. Coherence adds to the definition of quasicoherence the clause that $f(w) = w$. It follows from results in Fritz (2017, pp. 212–213) that:

Proposition 3.6.4 *If $\approx$ is a quasicoherent equivalence system, then $\mathfrak{F}_\approx$ is a* VDRF.

With this concrete way of constructing variable domain frames, we can easily show that both the Barcan formula Bc and its converse have instances which are not valid on VDRFs. This is expected, as these formulas are hallmarks of (propositional) necessitism; see Williamson (2013, chapter 2) for discussion. To state these observations, note that on frames with a universal accessibility relation, the following definition allows us to state in the object language that the proposition expressed by any given formula φ exists, in the sense of being in the domain of the world of evaluation:

$E\varphi := \exists q\square(q \leftrightarrow \varphi),$

where q is chosen to be some variable which is not free in φ.

Proposition 3.6.5 *The following instances of* Bc *and its converse are not valid on* VDRF*s:*

(1) $\forall p\square\square Ep \rightarrow \square\forall p\square Ep$
(2) $\square\forall pEp \rightarrow \forall p\square Ep$

Proof Let $\approx$ be the equivalence system based on $\{1,2,3\}$ such that $v \approx_w u$ if and only if $v = u$, or $w = 1$ and $\{v,u\} \subseteq \{2,3\}$. $\approx$ is coherent, so $\mathfrak{F}_{\approx}$ is a VDRF. (1) is false in 1, and (2) is false in 2. □

Since all instances of the converse of Bc are derivable in NPQMLs, it follows that the logic of VDRFs is not normal. In fact, even the logic of the class of frames $\mathfrak{F}_{\approx}$ for coherent equivalence systems $\approx$ – which includes the strong NML S5 – is not normal. The culprit is the rule of necessitation: although Ep is valid on VDRFs, its necessitation is not valid, as demonstrated by the frame used in the proof of Proposition 3.6.5.

The failure of necessitation creates difficulties for constructing axiomatic systems. One solution is to axiomatize the validities according to a more demanding notion of validity which removes the constraint on assignment functions, defined as follows:

$\mathfrak{F} \Vdash' \varphi$ if $\mathfrak{F}, w, a \Vdash \varphi$ for all $w \in W$ and $a: \Phi \rightarrow \mathcal{P}(W)$.

It is easy to see that questions about $\Vdash$-validity can straightforwardly be reduced to questions about $\Vdash'$-validity, as the following equivalence holds for any VDNF $\mathfrak{F}$ and formula φ with free variables $p_1, \ldots, p_n$:

$\mathfrak{F} \Vdash \varphi$ if and only if $\mathfrak{F} \Vdash' \forall p_1 \ldots \forall p_n\varphi$.

By axiomatizing the $\Vdash'$-validities of a class of frames, one thereby also obtains a syntactic characterization of the $\Vdash$-validities.

The $\Vdash'$-validities of any class of VDRFs are easily seen to be closed under necessitation, and therefore more amenable to a standard axiomatic treatment. However, they need not include all instances of the axiom schema UI; for example, $\forall pEp \rightarrow Ep$ is not $\Vdash'$-valid on the frame used in the proof of Proposition 3.6.5. To axiomatize the $\Vdash'$-validities of a class of VDRFs, one might therefore follow the model of axiomatizations of modal predicate logics based on variable domain frames, which are often based on axiom systems of free logic. Along the lines of the approach taken in Hughes and Cresswell (1996, chapter 16), one might restrict UI by an existence predicate. As we have seen, such a predicate E can be defined in the context of VDRFs with a single universal accessibility relation. The restricted version of UI can then be formulated as follows:

(RUI) $\forall p \varphi \to (E\psi \to \varphi[\psi/p])$ whenever ψ is free for p in φ.

The matter is more difficult in the context of VDRFs generally, or even VDNFs, where the definition of $E\varphi$ is not guaranteed to express existence of the relevant proposition. In these contexts, one might instead adopt the approach of Kripke (1963b), and use an axiom schema consisting of certain closed instances of UI:

(CUI) $\forall q(\forall p \varphi \to \varphi[q/p])$ whenever q is free for p in φ.

However, subtleties involving the permutation of quantifiers emerge on this approach; see Fine (1983) and Hughes and Cresswell (1996, pp. 304–309).

Whichever approach is taken, propositionally quantified modal logics also pose special difficulties in terms of axiomatizability. Recall from Section 2 that many classes of relational frames have a propositionally quantified modal logic which is not recursively enumerable. The case of relational frames with a universal accessibility relation emerged as an exception, as the propositionally quantified modal logic of this class of frames is decidable. Since quasicoherent equivalence systems are based on such frames, the question arises whether the resulting class of VDRFs has a recursively enumerable logic. Fritz (2017, pp. 211–212) shows that this is not the case, and the result extends to the class of coherent equivalence systems as well:

Proposition 3.6.6 *If* C *is the class of* VDRFs $\mathfrak{F}_\approx$, *for* $\approx$ *a quasicoherent/coherent equivalence system, then* $\mathcal{L}^\square$(C) *is recursively isomorphic to second-order logic.*

Equivalence systems can be expanded to accommodate nontrivial accessibility relations or neighborhood functions, a generalization which has not yet been investigated systematically. For an application of such structures to the logic of awareness, see Fritz and Lederman (2016). The resulting VDRFs can also be used to establish results concerning NPQMLs; for example, Ding (2021b) uses them to establish that $4^\vee$ is not derivable in $K_\Pi D45$, a result mentioned in Section 3.2.

There are also many open questions concerning variable domain frames beyond those determined by equivalence systems. One example appears to be the following:

Open Question 7 *Is the propositionally quantified modal logic of the class of all* VDRFs *recursively enumerable?*

As usual, there are a number of natural variations on this question, which also appear to be open. For example, we might ask about the logic of the class of VDNFs, and whether the answers to these questions depend on the modal signature.

3.7 Substitutional Quantifiers

In this section, we consider a *substitutional interpretation* of propositional quantifiers, on which a universal quantification is true just in case all of its substitution instances are true. Philosophical discussion of a substitutional interpretation of propositional quantifiers can be found especially in the debate on deflationism about truth, mentioned in Section 1.6; see, for example, Grover et al. (1975), van Inwagen (2002), and Christensen (2011). For an example of an application of propositional quantifiers – to the logic of necessity and apriority – which assumes a substitutional interpretation, see Tharp (1989). Here, we focus on how a substitutional interpretation of propositional quantifiers could be formalized model-theoretically.

In the context of relational or neighborhood frames, the intended truth conditions of a propositional quantifier on the substitutional interpretation are easy enough to state: $\forall p\varphi$ is intended to be true just in case $\varphi[\psi/p]$ is true for every $\psi \in \mathcal{L}^\sigma$ free for p in φ. However, it is well known that these truth conditions cannot serve the usual purpose of a recursive determination of which formulas are true relative to which worlds and assignment functions. To illustrate this, consider the case of the formula $\forall pp$. According to the truth conditions just stated, this is true if and only if every one of its substitution instances is true. But one of these substitution instances is $\forall pp$ itself, so one of the conditions for the truth of $\forall pp$ is the truth of $\forall pp$ itself.

There are different ways of solving this difficulty. One option is to limit the substitution instances, which is suggested by Grover (1972). For example, one might restrict the substitution instances to quantifier-free formulas, to Boolean combinations of proposition letters, or to just proposition letters. A substitutional interpretation of propositional quantifiers restricted to quantifier-free instances in the context of a logic of (un)awareness can be found in Halpern and Rêgo (2009), and a similar treatment of a quantified "public announcement" operator is investigated in Ågotnes et al. (2016). (See also van Ditmarsch (2023) for a general survey of work in dynamic epistemic logic involving operators which incorporate some aspect of propositional quantification, often involving restricted substitutional clauses.) These relatively straightforward treatments of substitutional quantifiers typically lead to logics which are non-classical, as not all instances of UI are guaranteed to be valid, similar to the logics mentioned briefly at the end of Section 3.5. There are various ways of trying to improve on these limitations. For example, Grover (1973) extends the capabilities of propositional quantifiers on a substitutional interpretation by stratifying propositional variables into an infinite hierarchy of levels, reminiscent of the ramified type theory of Whitehead and Russell (1910–13). Another example is Halpern and Rêgo (2013), whose refined models make the relevant substitution instances relative to the world of evaluation, in some ways similar to the variable domains discussed in Section 3.6.

There is, however, an alternative approach, which retains the truth conditions of substitutional propositional quantifiers as stated earlier. On this alternative approach, these truth conditions do not play a part in a recursive determination of truth, but serve as holistic constraints on admissible interpretation functions used to define the relevant class of models. Such a model construction is briefly mentioned by Bull (1969, p. 258), and considered in more detail by Gabbay (1971), who uses it to develop models for NPQMLs based on neighborhood frames. For present purposes, it suffices to illustrate the idea using models based on relational frames. Such models might take the form $\langle W, R_\square, \Vdash \rangle_{\square \in O}$, where $\langle W, R_\square \rangle_{\square \in O}$ is a relational frame. $\Vdash$ is then required to be a relation between members of W and formulas of $\mathcal{L}^\sigma$ satisfying the intended truth conditions. In the case of proposition letters and Boolean operators, these are the standard truth conditions stated in Definition 2.3.1. For propositional quantifiers, they are the substitutional truth conditions, which can be stated as follows:

$w \Vdash \forall p \varphi$ if and only if $w \Vdash \varphi[\psi/p]$ for all $\psi \in \mathcal{L}^\sigma$ free for p in φ.

On this approach, it is a substantial claim that there are any models at all. For a given relational frame, we cannot simply assume that there is any relation $\Vdash$ of truth satisfying the desired truth conditions. In certain cases, it can be shown that there is such a relation; for example, Kripke (1976, p. 332) notes that a suitable relation $\Vdash$ can always be found if all operators are truth-functional. This can be shown using the eliminability of propositional quantifiers in such a setting, discussed in Section 1.3. In the context of his models based on neighborhood frames, Gabbay (1971) establishes completeness results, which entail, for every formula φ which is not derivable in the relevant proof system, the existence of a model in which φ is falsified. It is important to note, however, that without an independent proof of the consistency of the relevant proof system, such a completeness result does not entail the existence of any model.

A substitutional interpretation of propositional quantifiers in modal logic is especially congenial on a substitutional interpretation of the modal operators. Such an interpretation of the unary operator □ was proposed by McKinsey (1945). On one elegant form of this proposal, □φ is true just in case any uniform substitution of the free variables in φ produces a true formula. Combined with the substitutional interpretation of quantifiers, this interpretation can be defined as follows:

Definition 3.7.1 *Let a* valuation *be a function v from* $\mathcal{L}^\square$ *to* $\{0,1\}$. *v is* substitutional *if it satisfies the following constraints, where* $p_1, \ldots, p_n$ *are the free variables in* φ:

$v(\perp) = 0$

$v(\varphi \rightarrow \psi) = 1$ *if and only if* $v(\varphi) = 1$ *only if* $v(\psi) = 1$

$v(\square\varphi) = 1$ *if and only if* $v(\varphi[\psi_1/p_1, \ldots, \psi_n/p_n]) = 1$ *for all* $\psi_1, \ldots, \psi_n \in \mathcal{L}^\square$
   free for $p_1, \ldots, p_n$, *respectively, in* φ

$v(\forall p\varphi) = 1$ *if and only if* $v(\varphi[\psi/p]) = 1$ *for all* $\psi \in \mathcal{L}^\square$ *free for p in* φ

At first glance, it might appear as if in the context of substitutional valuations, □φ becomes interchangeable with $\forall p_1 \ldots \forall p_1\varphi$, where $p_1, \ldots, p_n$ are the free variables in φ. For example, consider a formula φ with a single free variable p. Then the conditions for a valuation v to map □φ to 1 are the same as the conditions for v to map $\forall p\varphi$ to 1; namely, v must map $\varphi[\psi/p]$ to 1 for every ψ free for p in φ. However, this does not mean that we can eliminate □ using propositional quantifiers in the context of substitutional valuations. The reason is that there is a crucial *syntactic* difference between □φ and $\forall p\varphi$: the variable p remains free in □φ but not in $\forall p\varphi$. This means that the two formulas embed differently. For example, the constraints on substitutional valuations require $\forall p\neg\square p$ to be mapped to 0 but $\forall p\neg\forall pp$ to be mapped to 1.

Are there substitutional valuations of $\mathcal{L}^\square$? Even in the quantifier-free case, where we use $\mathcal{L}^\square_{qf}$ instead of $\mathcal{L}^\square$ and omit the last clause of Definition 3.7.1, it is far from clear that there are any substitutional valuations. In fact, the 42nd question on the list of questions in mathematical logic by Friedman (1975) asks whether there is a substitutional valuation in the quantifier-free case, with Friedman conjecturing that there is such a valuation. The existence of such a valuation was independently established by Prucnal (1979), and by Kit Fine in unpublished work. Fine's proof is to be published as part of Bacon and Fine (forthcoming). Friedman also asks whether there is a *unique* substitutional valuation which maps every $p \in \Phi$ to 1, and conjectures that the answer is negative. This further question on uniqueness remains open in the quantifier-free case.

More generally, one might ask whether every mapping from $p \in \Phi$ to $\{0,1\}$ has a unique extension to a substitutional valuation of $\mathcal{L}_{qf}^{\square}$. In the propositionally quantified case, all of these questions remain open:

Open Question 8 *Is there a substitutional valuation of $\mathcal{L}^{\square}$? If so, does every mapping from $p \in \Phi$ to $\{0,1\}$ have a unique extension to a substitutional valuation of $\mathcal{L}^{\square}$?*

Bacon and Fine (forthcoming) consider a version of this question, and conjecture that there is a substitutional valuation of $\mathcal{L}^{\square}$. It is worth noting that Bacon and Fine's definition of a substitutional valuation is slightly different, since their language contains both propositional variables and nonlogical constants, and their conditions for the modal operator and quantifier refer to closed substitution instances only. Moreover, while their constraints on quantified statements match the definition given here insofar as it considers substitutions of the bound propositional variable, their constraints on modal statements of the form $\square\varphi$ vary not the interpretation of free variables in φ but of the propositional constants in φ. This leads to substantial differences, even within the shared fragment of the language not involving any propositional constants. For example, in Bacon and Fine's setting, a substitutional valuation must map $(p \rightarrow \square p) \wedge (\neg p \rightarrow \square\neg p)$ to 1 (taking p to be a variable, as before), whereas on the definition presented here, it must map this formula to 0. It is also worth noting that it is not immediately obvious whether substitutional valuations as defined earlier verify all classical principles, that is, all theorems of C_{Π}. In contrast, in the quantifier-free case, it follows from results of McKinsey (1945) that any substitutional valuation verifies every theorem of S4M. If the answer to the first part of Question 8 is positive, there are therefore natural follow-up questions concerning which logical principles are guaranteed to be verified by substitutional valuations, and whether there are substitutional valuations which verify, for example, every theorem of $S_{\Pi}4M$.

4 Conclusion

We have seen that propositional quantifiers constitute a natural extension of a number of logical systems, in particular propositional modal logics. The resulting propositionally quantified modal logics can be interpreted over many well-known classes of models for propositional modal logics. Many of the standard questions concerning propositional modal logics arise as well for propositionally quantified modal logics. Some results extend from the standard quantifier-free setting to the setting with propositional quantifiers, but often they do not do so, or do not do so without nontrivial adjustments. Over many classes of models, propositional quantifiers constitute a substantial addition, with further classes of models becoming definable and the logics of various classes of models increasing in computational complexity, in a significant number of cases becoming not recursively axiomatizable.

Almost all of the models discussed in this Element effectively represent propositions as elements of a Boolean algebra: They either explicitly start from a Boolean algebra, or are based on a set of worlds W and effectively represent propositions as elements of a field of sets $A \subseteq \mathcal{P}(W)$. Even the purely substitutional interpretation considered in Section 3.7, in which sentences are only assigned 0 or 1, can be thought of as based on a conception of the propositions as truth-values, and so as the elements of the two-element Boolean algebra. The fact that all of our models operate with an underlying algebra which is Boolean plays a role in ensuring that the logics to which they give rise are classical. For example, if the underlying algebra is Boolean, then every tautology is always interpreted as the top element 1 of the algebra, and so valid on the relevant model. However, it is important to be clear that making the underlying algebra Boolean is not *dictated* by the constraints of classicality.

To illustrate this very abstractly, consider again the notion of a BAE-matrix $\mathfrak{M} = \langle A, 0, \beth, F, *_o \rangle_{o \in O}$, stated in Definition 3.3.4. The definition of a BAE-matrix requires $\langle A, 0, \beth \rangle$ to be a Boolean algebra, and F to be a filter. This ensures that every tautology is interpreted as 1, and so as a member of F, which in turn means that tautologies are valid. But we might also impose this requirement more directly: We might simply let $\langle A, 0, \beth \rangle$ be an arbitrary algebraic structure, with 0 a nullary and $\beth$ a binary function, while requiring that $0 \notin F$ and $x \beth y \in F$ just in case $x \in F$ only if $y \in F$. This will also guarantee that all tautologies are members of F, and thereby guarantee the validity of tautologies. This abstract algebraic approach can be extended to quantifiers; for an example, see Lewitzka (2015). There are many variations on this general idea; for another example in the more general context of higher-order logic, see Muskens (2007).

Considering these more general algebraic models is especially natural in exploring theories of propositional identity. We have not specifically considered an identity connective here, but such a connective does fall under the general notion of a modal operator we have been working with: we can think of a propositional identity connective = simply as a binary modal operator, in the wide sense of modality employed here. Such an identity *operator* may be unfamiliar, but it has many interesting applications. For example, as mentioned in Section 1.6, a version of the Epimenides paradox is naturally formalized using propositional quantifiers.

To illustrate this, let E be an operator formalizing "is said by Epimenides". Assume that Epimenides says that everything Epimenides says is false. That is, assume $E\delta$, where δ is the following sentence:

(δ) $\forall p(Ep \rightarrow \neg p)$

Is everything Epimenides says false? That is, δ? Instantiating δ with δ, we obtain:

(γ) $E\delta \rightarrow \neg\delta$

We assumed $E\delta$, so $\neg\delta$ follows, but this contradicts the assumption. So, $\neg\delta$. But then there is some p such that Ep and p. What is this p? It cannot be δ, since $\neg\delta$. But we have only assumed that Epimenides says δ. We seem to be forced, paradoxically, to the conclusion that there is *something else* which Epimenides says, even if he only utters "$\forall p(Ep \rightarrow \neg p)$":

(β) $\neg\forall q(Eq \leftrightarrow q = \delta)$

As the present sketch suggests, this argument can be carried out in a relatively weak propositionally quantified modal logic, using plausible deductive principles for $=$ and no particular assumptions about E. This was well known to the founders of symbolic logic, and a derivation along these lines can be found, for example, in Hilbert and Ackermann (1938, pp. 114–121). The paradox, in its formalization using propositional quantifiers, was also discussed at length by the pioneer of propositional quantifiers, Prior (1958b, 1961).

In the presence of a modality of necessity $\Box$, applying necessitation and existential generalization to β yields the following corollary:

(α) $\exists p\neg\Diamond\forall q(Eq \leftrightarrow (q = p))$

Thus, there is something – δ – which Epimenides cannot uniquely say. Various alternative interpretations of E yield other paradoxical conclusions. For example, we might read E as "is entertained", and conclude that there is some proposition, namely the proposition that everything entertained is false, which cannot be uniquely entertained. This modal version of the paradox was also noted by Kaplan (1995), who observed the validity of α on a very general class of possible worlds models. Kaplan described this observation as a problem for possible world *semantics*. However, as pointed out by Anderson (2009) and Lindström (2009), the *deducibility* of this principle from plausible axiomatic principles shows that the problem is not obviously tied to any particular model theory. The issue has recently received renewed attention; see Bacon et al. (2016), Holliday and Litak (2018), Bacon and Uzquiano (2018), Ding and Holliday (2020), and Uzquiano (2021).

Returning to non-Boolean models, such models are especially interesting for exploring views on which propositions are very finely individuated. However, we need to be cautious in doing so, for two reasons: First, once we reject the identities of Boolean algebras, we must reconsider the interdefinability of the operators $\top$, $\bot$, $\neg$, $\wedge$, $\vee$, $\rightarrow$ and $\leftrightarrow$. For example, on a fine-grained conception of propositions, the formulas $(p \rightarrow \bot) \rightarrow q$ and $(q \rightarrow \bot) \rightarrow p$ may not always express the same proposition (on a given interpretation of p and q). In such a situation, it is not clear that we can use $(\varphi \rightarrow \bot) \rightarrow \psi$ to abbreviate $\varphi \vee \psi$: the former may simply fail to express disjunction. In fact, in such a setting, it is not clear that we can make any such abbreviations. We may then have to take all of the operators as primitive.

Second, the restrictiveness of languages like $\mathcal{L}^\sigma$ involving only propositional quantifiers may make fine-grained theories of propositions more plausible than they are. This is because prima facie plausible principles of fine individuation of propositions can be shown to be inconsistent using higher-order quantifiers, by an argument due to Russell (1903, appendix B) and Myhill (1958). In a higher-order language, using X and Y as variables which take the position of unary sentential operators, a natural version of the idea that propositions are structured leads to the following principle:

$$\forall X \forall Y \forall p (Xp = Yp \rightarrow X = Y)$$

This, however, can be shown to be inconsistent in a natural proof system of classical third-order logic, using the argument of Russell and Myhill. Since the argument cannot be formulated in a purely propositionally quantified modal language, limiting ourselves to such languages may therefore make various theories of propositional identification seem more attractive than they actually are. As discussed in Section 1.4, the restrictiveness of languages like $\mathcal{L}^\sigma$ has both advantages and disadvantages. It may well be that for the purpose of exploring theories of propositional identity, it is better to work in richer languages. Such languages need not necessarily provide a full infinite hierarchy of types. For example, in Fritz (2023c) I develop a theory of propositional identity using a fragment of third-order logic which includes propositional quantifiers alongside quantifiers binding variables in the position of sentential operators.

Is a structured theory of propositions consistent in a merely propositionally quantified setting? The consistency question is most naturally posed as concerning a logic of propositional identity which consists of just the elementary principles of identity:

(RI) $p = p$

(LL) $p = q \rightarrow (\varphi \rightarrow \varphi[q/p])$, whenever q is free for p in φ

For any modal signature $\sigma = \langle O, \rho \rangle$ which includes the binary identity connective =, let I^σ be C_Π^σRILL, the classical propositionally quantified modal logic axiomatized by RI and LL. A natural theory of structured propositions can be formulated using the following schemas, where μ and v may be any propositional connective (i.e., Boolean operator or member of O):

(S$_1$) $\mu p_1 \ldots p_n \neq v q_1 \ldots q_m$, whenever μ and v are distinct

(S$_2$) $\mu p_1 \ldots p_n = \mu q_1 \ldots q_n \rightarrow p_i = q_i$

To illustrate these two principles: By S$_1$, no conditional proposition is an identity proposition. By S$_2$, conditional propositions can only be identical if their antecedents are the same and their consequents are the same. It follows immediately from observations in Fritz (2023b) that S$_1$ and S$_2$ are jointly consistent in I^σ. What is not obvious is whether we can introduce corresponding principles for propositional quantifiers:

(S$_3$) $\mu p_1 \ldots p_n \neq \forall q \varphi$

(S$_4$) $\forall p \varphi = \forall p \psi \rightarrow \forall p(\varphi = \psi)$

In the presence of higher-order quantifiers, S$_1$ – S$_4$ are jointly inconsistent; indeed, Church (1984) essentially notes that S$_4$ is inconsistent by itself. (See also Fritz (2023a,b) for discussion of a number of variant principles of propositional structure and their consistency.) In a more restricted language like $\mathcal{L}^\sigma$, consistency appears to be an open question.

In the course of the journey through the landscape of logics with propositional quantifiers which this Element has taken, we have seen many areas calling for further development. I have highlighted some examples of particularly intriguing open questions in the hope of inspiring others to explore propositional quantifiers, especially in the context of modal logics. It therefore seems fitting to conclude with a final open question:

Open Question 9 *Are* S$_1$ – S$_4$ *jointly consistent in* I^σ *?*

Abbreviations

The following abbreviations are used with the following meanings, with page numbers in parentheses referring to the introduction of the relevant concept:

BAE: Boolean algebra expansion (p. 62)
CBAE: complete Boolean algebra expansion (p. 62)
CML: congruential modal logic (p. 53)
CPQML: congruential propositionally quantified modal logic (p. 53)
NML: normal modal logic (p. 31)
NPQML: normal propositionally quantified modal logic (p. 31)
QBAE: quantifiable Boolean algebra expansion (p. 72)
QGNF: quantifiable general neighborhood frame (p. 75)
QGRF: quantifiable general relational frame (p. 75)
QCML: quasi-congruential modal logic (p. 69)
QCPQML: quasi-congruential propositionally quantified modal logic (p. 69)
QNML: quasi-normal modal logic (p. 69)
QNPQML: quasi-normal propositionally quantified modal logic (p. 69)
VDNF: variable domain neighborhood frame (p. 81)
VDRF: variable domain relational frame (p. 81)

References

Ågotnes, T., H. van Ditmarsch, and T. French. The undecidability of quantified announcements. *Studia Logica*, 104:597–640, 2016.

Adams, Robert Merrihew. Actualism and thisness. *Synthese*, 49:3–41, 1981.

Anderson, Alan Ross. An intensional interpretation of truth-values. *Mind*, 81:348–371, 1972.

Anderson, Alan Ross, and Nuel D. Belnap, Jr. Enthymemes. *The Journal of Philosophy*, 58:713–723, 1961.

Anderson, Alan Ross, Nuel D. Belnap, Jr, and J. Michael Dunn. *Entailment: The Logic of Relevance and Necessity*, volume II. Princeton: Princeton University Press, 1992.

Anderson, C. Anthony. Bealer's *Quality and Concept. Journal of Philosophical Logic*, 16:115–164, 1987.

Anderson, C. Anthony. The lesson of Kaplan's paradox about possible world semantics. In Joseph Almog and Paolo Leonardi, editors, *The Philosophy of David Kaplan*, pages 85–92. Oxford: Oxford University Press, 2009.

Andrews, Peter B. A reduction of the axioms for the theory of propositional types. *Fundamenta Mathematicae*, 52:345–350, 1963.

Antonelli, G. Aldo. and Richmond H. Thomason. Representability in second-order propositional poly-modal logic. *The Journal of Symbolic Logic*, 67:1039–1054, 2002.

Arló Costa, Horacio. First order extensions of classical systems of modal logic: The role of the Barcan schemas. *Studia Logica*, 71:87–118, 2002.

Baaz, Matthias, and Norbert Preining. Quantifier elimination for quantified propositional logics on Kripke frames of type ω. *Journal of Logic and Computation*, 18:649–668, 2008.

Baaz, Matthias, and Helmut Veith. An axiomatization of quantified propositional Gödel logic using the Takeuti–Titani rule. In Samuel R. Buss, Petr Hájek, and Pavel Pudlák, editors, Logic Colloquium '98, volume 13 of Lecture Notes in Logic, pages 91–104. Cambridge: Cambridge University Press, 2000.

Baaz, Matthias, Agata Ciabattoni, and Richard Zach. Quantified propositional Gödel logics. In Michel Parigot and Andrei Voronkov, editors, *Logic for Programming and Automated Reasoning. 7th International Conference, LPAR 2000*, volume 1955 of Lecture Notes in Artificial Intelligence, pages 240–256. Berlin: Springer, 2000.

Bacon, Andrew. *A Philosophical Introduction to Higher-Order Logics*. New York: Routledge, 2024.

Bacon, Andrew, and Kit Fine. The logic of logical necessity. In Romina Padró and Yale Weiss, editors, *Saul Kripke on Modal Logic*. Springer, forthcoming.

Bacon, Andrew, and Gabriel Uzquiano. Some results on the limits of thought. *Journal of Philosophical Logic*, 47:991–999, 2018.

Bacon, Andrew, John Hawthorne, and Gabriel Uzquiano. Higher-order free logic and the Prior–Kaplan paradox. *Canadian Journal of Philosophy*, 46:493–541, 2016.

Badia, Guillermo. Incompactness of the $\forall_1$ fragment of basic second-order propositional relevant logic. *Australasian Journal of Logic*, 16:1–8, 2019.

Barcan, Ruth C. A functional calculus of first order based on strict implication. *The Journal of Symbolic Logic*, 11:1–16, 1946.

Barcan, Ruth C. The identity of individuals in a strict functional calculus of second order. *The Journal of Symbolic Logic*, 12:12–15, 1947.

Bayart, Arnould. La correction de la logique modale du premier et second ordre S5. *Logique et Analyse*, 1:28–44, 1958.

Bayart, Arnould. Quasi-adéquation de la logique modale de second ordre S5 et adéquation de la logique modale de premier ordre S5. *Logique et Analyse*, 2:99–121, 1959.

Bealer, George. Property theory: The type-free approach v. the Church approach. *Journal of Philosophical Logic*, 23:139–171, 1994.

Bealer, George. Propositions. *Mind*, 107:1–32, 1998.

Becker, Oskar. Zur Logik der Modalitäten. *Jahrbuch für Philosophie und phänomenologische Forschung*, 11:497–548, 1930.

Belardinelli, Francesco. Hans van Ditmarsch, and Wiebe van der Hoek. Second-order propositional announcement logic. In John Thangarajah, Karl Tuyls, Catholijn Jonker, and Stacy Marsella, editors, *Proceedings of the 15th International Conference on Autonomous Agents and Multiagent Systems (AAMAS 2016)*, pages 635–643. New York: Association for Computing Machinery, 2016.

Belardinelli, Francesco. Wiebe van der Hoek, and Louwe B. Kuijer. Second-order propositional modal logic: Expressiveness and completeness results. *Artificial Intelligence*, 263:3–45, 2018.

Besnard, Philippe. Jean-Marc Guinnebault, and Emmanuel Mayer. Propositional quantification for conditional logic. In Dov M. Gabbay, Rudolf Kruse, Andreas Nonnengart, and Hans Jürgen Ohlbach, editors, *Qualitative and Quantitative Practical Reasoning*, Lecture Notes in Computer Science 1244, pages 183–197. Berlin: Springer, 1997.

Blackburn, Patrick. Maarten de Rijke, and Yde Venema. *Modal Logic*, volume 53 of Cambridge Tracts in Theoretical Computer Science. Cambridge: Cambridge University Press, 2001.

Blackburn, Patrick. Torben Braüner, and Julie Lundbak Kofod. Remarks on hybrid modal logic with propositional quantifiers. In Peter Hasle, David Jakobsen, and Peter Øhrstrøm, editors, *The Metaphysics of Time: Themes from Prior*, pages 401–426. Aalborg: Aalborg Universitetsforlag, 2020.

Boolos, George. To be is to be a value of a variable (or to be some values of some variables). *The Journal of Philosophy*, 81:430–449, 1984.

Boolos, George. *The Logic of Provability*. Cambridge: Cambridge University Press, 1985.

Bradfield, Julian. and Colin Stirling. Modal μ-calculi. In Patrick Blackburn, Johan van Benthem, and Frank Wolter, editors, *Handbook of Modal Logic*, pages 721–756. Amsterdam: Elsevier, 2007.

Brentano, Franz. *The True and the Evident*. London: Routledge and Kegan Paul, 1966.

Büchi, J. Richard. On a decision method in restricted second order arithmetic. In Ernest Nagel, Patrick Suppes, and Alfred Tarski, editors, *Logic, Methodology and Philosophy of Science: Proceedings of the 1960 International Congress*, pages 1–11. Redwood City, CA: Stanford University Press, 1962.

Bull, R. A. On possible worlds in propositional calculi. *Theoria*, 3:171–182, 1968.

Bull, R. A. On modal logics with propositional quantifiers. *The Journal of Symbolic Logic*, 34:257–263, 1969.

Carnap, Rudolf. *Introduction to Semantics*. Cambridge, MA: Harvard University Press, 1942.

Carnap, Rudolf. *Meaning and Necessity: A Study in Semantics and Modal Logic*. Chicago, IL: The University of Chicago Press, 1947.

Chagrov, Alexander. and Michael Zakharyaschev. *Modal Logic*, volume 35 of Oxford Logic Guides. Oxford: Clarendon Press, 1997.

Chellas, Brian F. *Modal Logic: An Introduction*. Cambridge: Cambridge University Press, 1980.

Christensen, Ryan. Propositional quantification. *Russell: The Journal of Bertrand Russell Studies*, 31:109–120, 2011.

Church, Alonzo. Review of *The Liar* by Alexandre Koyré. *The Journal of Symbolic Logic*, 11:131, 1946.

Church, Alonzo. *Introduction to Mathematical Logic*. Princeton, NJ: Princeton University Press, 1956.

Church, Alonzo. Mathematics and logic. In Ernest Nagel, Patrick Suppes, and Alfred Tarski, editors, *Logic, Methodology and Philosophy of Science.*

Proceedings of the 1960 International Congress, pages 181–186. Redwood City, CA: Stanford University Press, 1962.

Church, Alonzo. Russell's theory of identity of propositions. *Philosophia Naturalis*, 21:513–522, 1984.

Church, Alonzo. Referee reports on Fitch's "A Definition of Value". In Joe Salerno, editor, *New Essays on the Knowability Paradox*, pages 13–20. Oxford: Oxford University Press, 2009 [1945].

Cohen, L. Jonathan. Can the logic of indirect discourse be formalised? *The Journal of Symbolic Logic*, 22:225–232, 1957.

Copeland, B. Jack. Meredith, Prior, and the history of possible world semantics. *Synthese*, 150:373–397, 2006.

Cresswell, M. J. Arnould Bayart's modal completeness theorems. *Logique et Analyse*, 229:89–142, 2015.

Crossley, John N., and Lloyd Humberstone. The logic of "actually". *Reports on Mathematical Logic*, 8:11–29, 1977.

Davey, B. A. and H. A. Priestley. *Introduction to Lattices and Order*. Cambridge: Cambridge University Press, second edition, 2002.

deVries, Willem. Wilfrid Sellars. In Edward N. Zalta, editor, *The Stanford Encyclopedia of Philosophy*. Metaphysics Research Lab, Stanford University, 2020.

Ding, Yifeng. On the logics with propositional quantifiers extending S5Π. In Guram Bezhanishvili, Giovanna D'Agostino, George Metcalfe, and Thomas Studer, editors, *Advances in Modal Logic*, volume 12, pages 219–235. College Publications, 2018.

Ding, Yifeng. On the logic of belief and propositional quantification. *Journal of Philosophical Logic*, 50:1143–1198, 2021a.

Ding, Yifeng. *Propositional Quantification and Comparison in Modal Logic*. PhD thesis, University of California, Berkeley, 2021b.

Ding, Yifeng, and Wesley H. Holliday. Another problem in possible world semantics. In Nicola Olivetti, Rineke Verbrugge, and Sara Negri, editors, *Advances in Modal Logic*, volume 13. College Publications, 2020.

Dorr, Cian, John Hawthorne, and Juhani Yli-Vakkuri. *The Bounds of Possibility: Puzzles of Modal Variation*. Oxford: Oxford University Press, 2021.

Došen, Kosta. Duality between modal algebras and neighborhood frames. *Studia Logica*, 48:219–234, 1989.

Dugundji, James. *Topology*. Boston: Allyn and Bacon, 1966.

Dunn, J. Michael, and Gary M. Hardegree. *Algebraic Methods in Philosophical Logic*. Oxford: Clarendon Press, 2001.

Ferreira, Fernando. Comments on predicative logic. *Journal of Philosophical Logic*, 35:1–8, 2006.

Fine, Kit. *For some proposition and so many possible worlds*. PhD thesis, University of Warwick, 1969.

Fine, Kit. Propositional quantifiers in modal logic. *Theoria*, 36:336–346, 1970.

Fine, Kit. In so many possible worlds. *Notre Dame Journal of Formal Logic*, 13:516–520, 1972.

Fine, Kit. An incomplete logic containing S4. *Theoria*, 40:23–29, 1974.

Fine, Kit. Properties, propositions and sets. *Journal of Philosophical Logic*, 6:135–191, 1977.

Fine, Kit. Failures of the interpolation lemma in quantified modal logic. *The Journal of Symbolic Logic*, 44:201–206, 1979.

Fine, Kit. First-order modal theories II – Propositions. *Studia Logica*, 39:159–202, 1980.

Fine, Kit. The permutation principle in quantificational logic. *Journal of Philosophical Logic*, 12:33–37, 1983.

Fitch, Frederic B. A logical analysis of some value concepts. *The Journal of Symbolic Logic*, 28:135–142, 1963. Reprinted in Salerno (2009).

Fitting, Melvin. Interpolation for first-order S5. *The Journal of Symbolic Logic*, 67:621–634, 2002.

Frege, Gottlob. *Begriffsschrift, eine der arithmetischen nachgebildete Formelsprache des reinen Denkens*. Halle a. S.: Louis Nebert, 1879.

Frege, Gottlob. Über Begriff und Gegenstand. *Vierteljahresschrift für wissenschaftliche Philosophie*, 16:192–205, 1892.

Frege, Gottlob. *Posthumous Writings*. Oxford: Basil Blackwell, 1979. Edited by Hans Hermes, Friedrich Kambartel and Friedrich Kaulbart.

Frege, Gottlob. *Philosophical and Mathematical Correspondence*. Oxford: Basil Blackwell, 1980. Edited by Gottfried Gabriel, Hans Hermes, Friedrich Kambartel, Christian Thiel and Albert Veraart.

French, Tim. Bisimulation quantified modal logics: Decidability. In Guido Governatori, Ian Hodkinson, and Yde Venema, editors, *Advances in Modal Logic*, volume 6, pages 147–166. College Publications, 2006.

French, Tim, and Mark Reynolds. A sound and complete proof system for QPTL. In Philippe Balbiani, Nobu-Yuki Suzuki, Frank Wolter, and Michael Zakharyaschev, editors, *Advances in Modal Logic*, volume 4, pages 127–147. College Publications, 2003.

Friedman, Harvey. One hundred and two problems in mathematical logic. *The Journal of Symbolic Logic*, 40:113–129, 1975.

Fritz, Peter. Propositional contingentism. *The Review of Symbolic Logic*, 9:123–142, 2016.

Fritz, Peter. Logics for propositional contingentism. *The Review of Symbolic Logic*, 10:203–236, 2017.

Fritz, Peter. Propositional quantification in bimodal S5. *Erkenntnis*, 85:455–465, 2020.

Fritz, Peter. Propositional potentialism. In Federico L. G. Faroldi and Frederik Van De Putte, editors, *Kit Fine on Truthmakers, Relevance and Non-Classical Logic*, volume 26 of *Outstanding Contributions to Logic*, pages 469–502. Cham: Springer, 2023a.

Fritz, Peter. Operands and instances. *The Review of Symbolic Logic*, 16:188–209, 2023b.

Fritz, Peter. *The Foundations of Modality: From Propositions to Possible Worlds*. Oxford: Oxford University Press, 2023c.

Fritz, Peter. Axiomatizability of propositionally quantified modal logics on relational frames. *The Journal of Symbolic Logic*, forthcoming.

Fritz, Peter. Nonconservative extensions by propositional quantifiers and modal incompleteness. Unpublished.

Fritz, Peter, and Nicholas K. Jones, editors. *Higher-Order Metaphysics*. Oxford: Oxford University Press, 2024.

Fritz, Peter, and Harvey Lederman. Standard state space models of unawareness. *Electronic Proceedings in Theoretical Computer Science*, 215:141–158, 2016. Proceedings of the 15th Conference on Theoretical Aspects of Rationality and Knowledge (TARK 2015).

Gabbay, Dov M. Montague type semantics for modal logics with propositional quantifiers. *Zeitschrift für mathematische Logik und Grundlagen der Mathematik*, 17:245–249, 1971.

Gabbay, Dov M. On 2nd order intuitionistic propositional calculus with full comprehension. *Archiv für mathematische Logik und Grundlagenforschung*, 16:177–186, 1974.

Gallin, Daniel. *Intensional and Higher-Order Modal Logic*. Amsterdam: North-Holland, 1975.

Garson, James W. Quantification in modal logic. In Dov M. Gabbay and Franz Guenthner, editors, *Handbook of Philosophical Logic*, volume II, pages 249–307. Dordrecht: D. Reidel, 1st edition, 1984.

Gerson, Martin. An extension of S4 complete for the neighbourhood semantics but incomplete for the relational semantics. *Studia Logica*, 34:333–342, 1975a.

Gerson, Martin. The inadequacy of the neighbourhood semantics for modal logic. *The Journal of Symbolic Logic*, 40:141–148, 1975b.

Gerson, Martin. A neighbourhood frame for T with no equivalent relational frame. *Zeitschrift für mathematische Logik und Grundlagen der Mathematik*, 22:29–34, 1976.

Ghilardi, Silvio, and Marek Zawadowski. Undefinability of propositional quantifiers in the modal system S4. *Studia Logica*, 55:259–271, 1995.

Givant, Steven, and Paul Halmos. *Introduction to Boolean Algebras*. New York: Springer, 2009.

Goldblatt, Robert. The McKinsey axiom is not canonical. *The Journal of Symbolic Logic*, 56:554–562, 1991.

Goldblatt, Robert. *Quantifiers, Propositions and Identity. Admissible Semantics for Quantified Modal and Substructural Logics*. Cambridge: Cambridge University Press, 2011.

Goldblatt, Robert, and Michael Kane. An admissible semantics for propositionally quantified relevant logic. *Journal of Philosophical Logic*, 39:73–100, 2010.

Grover, Dorothy L. *Topics in Propositional Quantification*. PhD thesis, University of Pittsburgh, 1970.

Grover, Dorothy L. Propositional quantifiers. *Journal of Philosophical Logic*, 1:111–136, 1972. Reprinted in Grover (1992).

Grover, Dorothy L. Propositional quantification and quotation contexts. In Hugues Leblanc, editor, *Truth, Syntax and Modality*, pages 101–110. Amsterdam: North-Holland, 1973.

Grover, Dorothy L. *A Prosentential Theory of Truth*. Princeton: Princeton University Press, 1992.

Grover, Dorothy L., Joseph L. Camp, Jr., and Nuel D. Belnap, Jr. A prosentential theory of truth. *Philosophical Studies*, 27:73–125, 1975. Reprinted in Grover (1992).

Gurevich, Yuri, and Saharon Shelah. Monadic theory of order and topology in ZFC. *Annals of Mathematical Logic*, 23:179–198, 1983.

Gärdenfors, Peter. On the extensions of S5. *Notre Dame Journal of Formal Logic*, 414:277–280, 1973.

Gödel, Kurt. Über formal unentscheidbare Sätze der Principia Mathematica und verwandter Systeme I. *Monatshefte für Mathematik und Physik*, 38:173–198, 1931.

Halbach, Volker, and Philip Welch. Necessities and necessary truths: A prolegomenon to the use of modal logic in the analysis of intensional notions. *Mind*, 118:71–100, 2009.

Halmos, Paul, and Steven Givant. *Logic as Algebra*. The Mathematical Association of America, 1998.

Halpern, Joseph Y., and Leandro C. Rêgo. Reasoning about knowledge of unawareness. *Games and Economic Behaviour*, 67:503–525, 2009.

Halpern, Joseph Y., and Leandro C. Rêgo. Reasoning about knowledge of unawareness revisited. *Mathematical Social Sciences*, 65:73–84, 2013.

Hansson, Bengt, and Peter Gärdenfors. A guide to intensional semantics. In *Modality, Morality and Other Problems of Sense and Nonsense: Essays dedicated to Sören Halldén*, pages 151–167. Lund: CWK Gleerup Bokförlag, 1973.

Hawthorne, John. *Knowledge and Lotteries*. Oxford: Clarendon Press, 2004.

Heidelberger, Herbert. The indispensability of truth. *American Philosophical Quarterly*, 5:212–217, 1968.

Henkin, Leon. Completeness in the theory of types. *The Journal of Symbolic Logic*, 15:81–91, 1950.

Henkin, Leon. A theory of propositional types. *Fundamenta Mathematicae*, 52:323–344, 1963.

Hilbert, D., and W. Ackermann. *Grundzüge der theoretischen Logik*. Berlin: Springer, second edition, 1938.

Holliday, Wesley H. A note on algebraic semantics for S5 with propositional quantifiers. *Notre Dame Journal of Formal Logic*, 60:311–332, 2019.

Holliday, Wesley H. Possibility semantics. In Melvin Fitting, editor, *Selected Topics from Contemporary Logics*, pages 363–476. London: College Publications, 2021.

Holliday, Wesley H. Possibility frames and forcing for modal logic. *The Australasian Journal of Logic*, forthcoming.

Holliday, Wesley H., and Tadeusz Litak. One modal logic to rule them all? In Guram Bezhanishvili, Giovanna D'Agostino, George Metcalfe, and Thomas Studer, editors, *Advances in Modal Logic*, volume 12, pages 367–386. College Publications, 2018.

Hughes, G. E., and M. J. Cresswell. *A New Introduction to Modal Logic*. London: Routledge, 1996.

Humberstone, Lloyd. From worlds to possibilities. *Journal of Philosophical Logic*, 10:313–339, 1981.

Jónnson, Bjarni, and Alfred Tarski. Boolean algebras with operators, part I. *American Journal of Mathematics*, 73:891–939, 1951.

Jónnson, Bjarni, and Alfred Tarski. Boolean algebras with operators, part II. *American Journal of Mathematics*, 74:127–162, 1952.

Kaminski, Michael, and Michael Tiomkin. The expressive power of second-order propositional modal logic. *Notre Dame Journal of Formal Logic*, 37:35–43, 1996.

Kaplan, David. S5 with multiple possibility. *The Journal of Symbolic Logic*, 35:355–356, 1970a.

Kaplan, David. S5 with quantifiable propositional variables. *The Journal of Symbolic Logic*, 35:355, 1970b.

Kaplan, David. Demonstratives. In Joseph Almog, John Perry, and Howard Wettstein, editors, *Themes from Kaplan*, pages 481–563. Oxford: Oxford University Press, 1989 [1977]. Completed and circulated in mimeograph in the published form in 1977.

Kaplan, David. A problem in possible-world semantics. In Walter Sinnott-Armstrong, Diana Raffman, and Nicholas Asher, editors, *Modality, Morality, and Belief*, pages 41–52. Cambridge: Cambridge University Press, 1995.

Kesten, Yonit, and Amir Pnueli. Complete proof system for QPTL. *Journal of Logic and Computation*, 12:701–745, 2002.

Koyré, Alexandre. The liar. *Philosophy and Phenomenological Research*, 6:344–362, 1946.

Kreisel, Georg. Monadic operators defined by means of propositional quantification in intuitionistic logic. *Reports on Mathematical Logic*, 12:9–15, 1981.

Kremer, Philip. Quantifying over propositions in relevance logic: Nonaxiomatisability of primary interpretations of $\forall p$ and $\exists p$. *The Journal of Symbolic Logic*, 58:334–349, 1993.

Kremer, Philip. Defining relevant implication in a propositionally quantified S4. *The Journal of Symbolic Logic*, 62:1057–1069, 1997a.

Kremer, Philip. On the complexity of propositional quantification in intuitionistic logic. *The Journal of Symbolic Logic*, 62:529–544, 1997b.

Kremer, Philip. Propositional quantification in the topological semantics for S4. *Notre Dame Journal of Formal Logic*, 38:295–313, 1997c.

Kremer, Philip. Completeness of second-order propositional S4 and H in topological semantics. *The Review of Symbolic Logic*, 11:507–518, 2018.

Kripke, Saul A. A completeness theorem in modal logic. *The Journal of Symbolic Logic*, 24:1–14, 1959.

Kripke, Saul A. Semantical analysis of modal logic I: Normal modal propositional calculi. *Zeitschrift für mathematische Logik und Grundlagen der Mathematik*, 9:67–96, 1963a.

Kripke, Saul A. Semantical considerations on modal logic. *Acta Philosophica Fennica*, 16:83–94, 1963b.

Kripke, Saul A. Semantical analysis of modal logic II: Non-normal modal propositional calculi. In J . W. Addison, Leon Henkin, and Alfred Tarski, editors,

The Theory of Models. Proceedings of the 1963 International Symposium at Berkeley, pages 206–220. Amsterdam: North-Holland, 1965.

Kripke, Saul A. Review of *Algebraic semantics for modal logics II* by E. J. Lemmon. *Mathematical Reviews*, 0205835 (34 #5661), 1967.

Kripke, Saul A. Is there a problem about substitutional quantification? In Gareth Evans and John McDowell, editors, *Truth and Meaning: Essays in Semantics*, pages 325–419. Oxford: Clarendon Press, 1976.

Kripke, Saul A. *Naming and Necessity*. Cambridge, MA: Harvard University Press, 1980 [1972]. First published in *Semantics of Natural Language*, edited by Donald Davidson and Gilbert Harman, pages 253–355, 763–769, Dordrecht: D. Reidel, 1972.

Kripke, Saul A. Review of *Failures of the interpolation lemma in quantified modal logic* by Kit Fine. *The Journal of Symbolic Logic*, 48:486–488, 1983.

Kuhn, Steven. A simple embedding of T into double S5. *Notre Dame Journal of Formal Logic*, 45:13–18, 2004.

Künne, Wolfgang. *Conceptions of Truth*. Oxford: Clarendon Press, 2003.

Lemmon, E. J. *The "Lemmon Notes". An Introduction to Modal Logic*. Oxford: Basil Blackwell, 1977 [1966]. In collaboration with Dana Scott, edited by Krister Segerberg, completed and circulated in 1966.

Lewis, Clarence Irving, and Cooper Harold Langford. *Symbolic Logic*. New York, NY: Dover, second edition, 1959 [1932]. Republication of the first edition published by The Century Company in 1932.

Lewis, David. *Counterfactuals*. Oxford: Basil Blackwell, 1973.

Lewitzka, Steffen. Denotational semantics for modal systems S3–S5 extended by axioms for propositional quantifiers and identity. *Studia Logica*, 103:507–544, 2015.

Lesniewski, Stanisław. Grundzüge eines neuen Systems der Grundlagen der Mathematik. *Fundamenta Mathematicae*, 14:1–81, 1929.

Lindström, Sten. Possible worlds semantics and the liar. In Joseph Almog and Paolo Leonardi, editors, *The Philosophy of David Kaplan*, pages 93–108. Oxford: Oxford University Press, 2009.

Litak, Tadeusz. Modal incompleteness revisited. *Studia Logica*, 76:329–342, 2004.

Lokhorst, Gert-Jan C. Propositional quantifiers in deontic logic. In Lou Goble and John-Jules Meyer, editors, *Deontic Logic and Artificial Normative Systems, DEON 2006*, volume 4048 of Lecture Notes in Artificial Intelligence, pages 201–209. Berlin: Springer, 2006.

Łoś, Jerzy. Logiki wielowartościowe a formalizacja funkcji intensjonalnych. *Kwartalnik Filozoficzny*, 17:59–78, 1948.

Łukasiewicz, Jan. On variable functors of propositional arguments. *Proceedings of the Royal Irish Academy*, 54:25–35, 1951.

Łukasiewicz, Jan, and Alfred Tarski. Untersuchungen über den Aussagenkalkül. *Comptes Rendus des séances de la Societé des Sciences et des Lettres de Varsovie*, 23:30–50, 1930. Reprinted in English translation by J. H. Woodger as "Investigations into the Sentential Calculus" in Alfred Tarski, *Logic, Semantics, Metamathematics*, pages 38–59, Oxford: Clarendon Press, 1956.

Löb, M. H. Embedding first order predicate logic in fragments of intuitionistic logic. *The Journal of Symbolic Logic*, 41:705–718, 1976.

Löwenheim, Leopold. Über Möglichkeiten im Relativkalkül. *Mathematische Annalen*, 76:447–470, 1915.

MacNeille, H. M. Partially ordered sets. *Transactions of the American Mathematical Society*, 42:416–460, 1937.

Makinson, David. On some completeness theorems in modal logic. *Zeitschrift für mathematische Logik und Grundlagen der Mathematik*, 12:379–384, 1966.

Makinson, David. Some embedding theorems for modal logic. *Notre Dame Journal of Formal Logic*, 12:252–254, 1971.

Makinson, David. A warning about the choice of primitive operators in modal logic. *Journal of Philosophical Logic*, 2:193–196, 1973.

McKinsey, J. C. C. A solution of the decision problem for the Lewis systems S2 and S4, with an application to topology. *The Journal of Symbolic Logic*, 6:117–134, 1941.

McKinsey, J. C. C. On the syntactical construction of systems of modal logic. *The Journal of Symbolic Logic*, 10:83–94, 1945.

McKinsey, J. C. C., and Alfred Tarski. The algebra of topology. *Annals of Mathematics*, 45:141–191, 1944.

McKinsey, J. C. C., and Alfred Tarski. Some theorems about the sentential calculi of Lewis and Heyting. *The Journal of Symbolic Logic*, 13:1–15, 1948.

Menzel, Christopher. Pure logic and "higher-order" metaphysics. In Peter Fritz and Nicholas K. Jones, editors, *Higher-Order Metaphysics*. Oxford: Oxford University Press, 2024.

Menzel, Christopher, and Edward N. Zalta. The fundamental theorem of world theory. *Journal of Philosophical Logic*, 43:333–363, 2014.

Meredith, C. A. On an extended system of the propositional calculus. *Proceedings of the Royal Irish Academy*, 54:37–47, 1951.

Montague, Richard. Universal grammar. *Theoria*, 36:373–398, 1970.

Muskens, Reinhard. Intensional models for the theory of types. *The Journal of Symbolic Logic*, 72:98–118, 2007.

Myhill, John. On the interpretation of the sign '⊃'. *The Journal of Symbolic Logic*, 18:60–62, 1953.

Myhill, John. Review of *Formal Logic* by A. N. Prior. *The Philosophical Review*, 66:117–120, 1957.

Myhill, John. Problems arising in the formalization of intensional logic. *Logique et Analyse*, 1:78–83, 1958.

Nagle, Michael C., and S. K. Thomason. The extensions of the modal logic K5. *The Journal of Symbolic Logic*, 50:102–109, 1985.

Pacuit, Eric. *Neighborhood Semantics for Modal Logic*. Short Textbooks in Logic. Cham: Springer, 2017.

Parry, W. T. Zum Lewisschen Aussagenkalkül. *Ergebnisse eines Mathematischen Kolloquiums*, 4:15–16, 1933.

Pascucci, Matteo. Propositional quantifiers in labelled natural deduction for normal modal logic. *Logic Journal of the IGPL*, 27:865–894, 2019.

Pitts, Andrew M. On an interpretation of second order quantification in first order intuitionistic propositional logic. *The Journal of Symbolic Logic*, 57:33–52, 1992.

Plantinga, Alvin. *The Nature of Necessity*. Oxford: Clarendon Press, 1974.

Połacik, Tomasz. Operators defined by propositional quantification and their interpretation over Cantor space. *Reports on Mathematical Logic*, 27:67–79, 1993.

Połacik, Tomasz. Pitts' quantifiers are not topological quantification. *Notre Dame Journal of Formal Logic*, 39:531–545, 1998a.

Połacik, Tomasz. Propositional quantification in the monadic fragment of intuitionistic logic. *The Journal of Symbolic Logic*, 63:269–300, 1998b.

Prawitz, Dag. *Natural Deduction. A Proof-Theoretical Study*, volume 3 of Stockhom Studies in Philosophy. Stockholm: Almqvist & Wiksell, 1965.

Prior, Arthur N. *Formal Logic*. Oxford: Clarendon Press, 1955.

Prior, Arthur N. *Time and Modality*. Oxford: Clarendon Press, 1957.

Prior, Arthur N. Escapism: the logical basis of ethics. In A. I. Melden, editor, *Essays in Moral Philosophy*. Seattle: University of Washington Press, 1958a.

Prior, Arthur N. Epimenides the Cretan. *The Journal of Symbolic Logic*, 23:261–266, 1958b.

Prior, Arthur N. On a family of paradoxes. *Notre Dame Journal of Formal Logic*, 2:16–32, 1961.

Prior, Arthur N. Wspólczesna logika w Anglii. *Ruch Filozoficzny*, 21:251–256, 1962.

Prior, Arthur N. *Past, Present and Future*. Oxford: Clarendon Press, 1967.

Prior, Arthur N. Egocentric logic. *Noûs*, 2:191–207, 1968.

Prior, Arthur N. *Objects of Thought*. Oxford: Clarendon Press, 1971. Edited by P. T. Geach and A. J. P. Kenny.

Prior, Arthur N., and Kit Fine. *Worlds, Times and Selves*. London: Duckworth, 1977.

Prucnal, Tadeusz. On two problems of Harvey Friedman. *Studia Logica*, 38:247–262, 1979.

Quine, W. V. *Philosophy of Logic*. Cambridge, MA: Harvard University Press, second edition, 1986 [1970]. First edition published in 1970.

Rabin, Michael O. Decidability of second-order theories and automata on infinite trees. *Transactions of the American Mathematical Society*, 141:1–35, 1969.

Ramsey, Frank P. Critical notice of *Tractatus Logico-Philosophicus* by Ludwig Wittgenstein. *Mind*, 32:465–478, 1923. Reprinted in Ramsey (1931).

Ramsey, Frank P. Facts and propositions. *Proceedings of the Aristotelian Society, Supplementary Volumes*, 7:153–170, 1927. Reprinted in Ramsey (1931).

Ramsey, Frank P. *The Foundations of Mathematics, and other Logical Essays*. London: Routledge and Kegan Paul, 1931. Edited by R. B. Braithwaite and G. E. Moore.

Ramsey, Frank P. *On Truth. Original Manuscript Materials (1927–1929) from the Ramsey Collection at the University of Pittsburgh*. Dordrecht: Kluwer, 1991. Edited by Nicholas Rescher and Ulrich Majer.

Rasiowa, Helena, and Roman Sikorski. *The Mathematics of Metamathematics*. Warsaw: Państwowe Wydawnictwo Naukowe, 1963.

Rönnedal, Daniel. Semantic tableau versions of some normal modal systems with propositional quantifiers. *Organon F*, 26:505–536, 2019.

Rönnedal, Daniel. The moral law and the good in temporal modal deontic logic with propositional quantifiers. *Australasian Journal of Logic*, 17:22–69, 2020.

Ross, Alf. Imperatives and logic. *Theoria*, 7:53–71, 1941.

Routley, Richard, and Robert K. Meyer. The semantics of entailment. In Hugues Leblanc, editor, *Truth, Syntax and Modality*, pages 199–243. Amsterdam: North-Holland, 1973.

Russell, Bertrand. *The Principles of Mathematics*. Cambridge: University Press, 1903.

Russell, Bertrand. The theory of implication. *American Journal of Mathematics*, 28:159–202, 1906.

Russell, Bertrand. Mathematical logic as based on the theory of types. *American Journal of Mathematics*, 30:222–262, 1908.

Russell, Bertrand. *Toward "Principia Mathematica". 1905–08*. The Collected Papers of Bertrand Russell. London: Routledge, 2014. Edited by Gregory H. Moore.

Salerno, Joe, editor. *New Essays on the Knowability Paradox*. Oxford: Oxford University Press, 2009.

Scott, Dana. Advice on modal logic. In Karel Lambert, editor, *Philosophical Problems in Logic. Some Recent Developments*, pages 143–173. Dordrecht: D. Reidel, 1970.

Scroggs, Schiller Joe. Extensions of the Lewis system S5. *The Journal of Symbolic Logic*, 16:112–120, 1951.

Segerberg, Krister. *An Essay in Classical Modal Logic*, volume 13 of Filosofiska Studier. Uppsala: Uppsala Universitet, 1971.

Segerberg, Krister. *Classical Propositional Operators. An Exercise in the Foundations of Logic*. Oxford: Clarendon Press, 1982.

Sellars, Wilfrid. Grammar and existence: A preface to ontology. *Mind*, 69:499–533, 1960.

Shapiro, Stewart. *Foundations without Foundationalism: A Case for Second-order Logic*. Oxford: Clarendon Press, 1991.

Shelah, Saharon. The monadic theory of order. *Annals of Mathematics*, 102:379–419, 1975.

Shukla, Ankit, Armin Biere, Martina Seidl, and Luca Pulina. A survey on applications of quantified boolean formulas. In *IEEE 31st International Conference on Tools with Artificial Intelligence (ICTAI 2019)*, pages 78–84. IEEE Computer Society, Conference Publishing Services, 2019.

Skvortsov, D. Non-axiomatizable second order intuitionistic propositional logic. *Annals of Pure and Applied Logic*, 86:33–46, 1997.

Sobolev, S. K. The intuitionistic propositional calculus with quantifiers (in Russian). *Matematicheskie Zametki*, 22:69–76, 1977.

Solovay, Robert M. Provability interpretations of modal logic. *Israel Journal of Mathematics*, 25:287–304, 1976.

Stalnaker, Robert. A theory of conditionals. In Nicholas Rescher, editor, *Studies in Logical Theory*, pages 98–112. Oxford: Blackwell, 1968.

Stalnaker, Robert. Possible worlds. *Noûs*, 10:65–75, 1976.

Stalnaker, Robert. *Mere Possibilities*. Princeton: Princeton University Press, 2012.

Steinsvold, Christopher. Some formal semantics for epistemic modesty. *Logic and Logical Philosophy*, 29:381–413, 2020.

Stone, M. H. The theory of representation for Boolean algebras. *Transactions of the American Mathematical Society*, 40:37–111, 1936.

Suszko, R. Review of *Many-Valued Logics and the Formalization of Intensional Functions* by Jerzy Łoś. *The Journal of Symbolic Logic*, 14:64–65, 1949.

Sørensen, Morten H. and Pawel Urzyczyn. A syntactic embedding of predicate logic into second-order propositional logic. *Notre Dame Journal of Formal Logic*, 51:457–473, 2010.

Tajtelbaum-Tarski, Alfred. O wyrazie pierwotnym logistyki. *Przegląd Filozoficzny*, 26:68–89, 1923. Reprinted in English translation by J. H. Woodger as "On the Primitive Term of Logistic" in Alfred Tarski, *Logic, Semantics, Metamathematics*, pages 1–23, Oxford: Clarendon Press, 1956.

Tang, Tsao-Chen. Algebraic postulates and a geometric interpretation for the Lewis calculus of strict implication. *Bulletin of the American Mathematical Society*, 44:737–744, 1938.

Tarski, Alfred. Zur Grundlegung der Bool'schen Algebra. *Fundamenta Mathematicae*, 24:177–198, 1935.

Tarski, Alfred. Über additive und multiplikative Mengenkörper und Mengenfunktionen. *Sprawozdania z Posiedzeń Towarzystwa Naukowego Warszawskiego, Wydział III Nauk Matematyczno-fizycznych (=Comptes Rendus des Séances de la Société des Sciences et des Lettres de Varsovie, Classe III)*, 30:151–181, 1937.

Tarski, Alfred. The concept of truth in formalized languages. In John Corcoran, editor, *Logic, Semantics, Metamathematics*, pages 152–278. Indianapolis: Hackett, 1983 [1933]. Translation of an article published in Polish in 1933 and German in 1935.

Tarski, Alfred. On the concept of following logically. *History and Philosophy of Logic*, 23:155–196, 2002 [1936]. Originally published in Polish and German in 1936.

ten Cate, Balder. Expressivity of second order propositional modal logic. *Journal of Philosophical Logic*, 35:209–223, 2006.

Tharp, Leslie. Three theorems of metaphysics. *Synthese*, 81:207–214, 1989.

Thomason, S. K. Semantic analysis of tense logics. *The Journal of Symbolic Logic*, 37:150–158, 1972.

Thomason, S. K. An incompleteness theorem in modal logic. *Theoria*, 40:30–34, 1974.

Thomason, S. K. Categories of frames for modal logic. *The Journal of Symbolic Logic*, 40:439–442, 1975.

Troelstra, A. S. On a second order propositional operator in intuitionistic logic. *Studia Logica*, 40:113–139, 1981.

Uzquiano, Gabriel. Elusive propositions. *Journal of Philosophical Logic*, 50:705–725, 2021.

van Benthem, Johan. *Modal Logic and Classical Logic*. Naples: Bibliopolis, 1983.

van Benthem, Johan, and Guram Bezhanishvili. Modal logics of space. In Marco Aiello, Ian Pratt-Hartmann, and Johan van Benthem, editors, *Handbook of Spatial Logics*, pages 217–298. Dordrecht: Springer, 2007.

van Ditmarsch, Hans. To be announced. *Information and Computation*, 292:1–42, 2023.

van Inwagen, Peter. Generalizations of homophonic truth-sentences. In Richard Schantz, editor, *What Is Truth?*, volume 1 of Current Issues in Theoretical Philosophy, pages 205–222. Berlin: De Gruyter, 2002.

Whitehead, Alfred North, and Bertrand Russell. *Principia Mathematica, Volumes 1–3*. Cambridge: Cambridge University Press, 1910–1913.

Williamson, Timothy. *Modal Logic as Metaphysics*. Oxford: Oxford University Press, 2013.

Williamson, Timothy. Menzel on pure logic and higher-order metaphysics. In Peter Fritz and Nicholas K. Jones, editors, *Higher-Order Metaphysics*. Oxford: Oxford University Press, 2024.

Wittgenstein, Ludwig. Logisch-philosophische Abhandlung. In Wilhelm Oswald, editor, *Annalen der Naturphilosophie*, volume 14, pages 185–262. Leipzig: Unesma, 1921.

Zach, Richard. Decidability of quantified propositional intuitionistic logic and S4 on trees of height and arity $\leq \omega$. *Journal of Philosophical Logic*, 33:155–164, 2004.

Zdanowski, Konrad. On second order intuitionistic propositional logic without a universal quantifier. *The Journal of Symbolic Logic*, 74:157–167, 2009.

Zhao, Zhiguang. Sahlqvist correspondence theory for second-order propositional modal logic. *Journal of Logic and Computation*, 33:577–598, 2023.

Acknowledgments

For questions, comments, and discussion, thanks to Andrew Bacon, Adam Bjorndahl, Sam Carter, Nevin Climenhaga, Yifeng Ding, Kit Fine, Salvatore Florio, Dmitri Gallow, Simon Goldstein, Jeremy Goodman, Wesley Holliday, Yipu Li, Gillian Russell, Juhani Yli-Vakkuri, and the participants at courses on propositional quantifiers at the Nordic Logic Summer School 2022 held at the University of Bergen, at NASSLLI 2022 held at the University of Southern California, at ESSLLI 2023 held at the University of Ljubljana, and at Beijing Normal University in 2022 and 2023. Special thanks to Valentin Goranko, Lloyd Humberstone, and two anonymous reviewers who read drafts and sent me detailed comments. Finally, I am grateful to the editors of the Logic and Philosophy series of Elements, Bradley Armour-Garb and Frederick Kroon, for the opportunity to publish in this series, and for their patience.

Cambridge Elements ☰

Philosophy and Logic

Bradley Armour-Garb
SUNY Albany

Bradley Armour-Garb is chair and Professor of Philosophy at SUNY Albany. His books include *The Law of Non-Contradiction* (co-edited with Graham Priest and J. C. Beall, 2004), *Deflationary Truth* and *Deflationism and Paradox* (both co-edited with J. C. Beall, 2005), *Pretense and Pathology* (with James Woodbridge, Cambridge University Press, 2015), *Reflections on the Liar* (2017), and *Fictionalism in Philosophy* (co-edited with Fred Kroon, 2020).

Frederick Kroon
The University of Auckland

Frederick Kroon is Emeritus Professor of Philosophy at the University of Auckland. He has authored numerous papers in formal and philosophical logic, ethics, philosophy of language, and metaphysics, and is the author of *A Critical Introduction to Fictionalism* (with Stuart Brock and Jonathan McKeown-Green, 2018).

About the Series

This Cambridge Elements series provides an extensive overview of the many and varied connections between philosophy and logic. Distinguished authors provide an up-to-date summary of the results of current research in their fields and give their own take on what they believe are the most significant debates influencing research, drawing original conclusions.

Cambridge Elements ☰

Philosophy and Logic

Printed in the United States
by Baker & Taylor Publisher Services